The Christian Heritage
God's Answers for a Searching World
Revised and Expanded

Floyd Bland

© 2008, 2014, 2017, 2022 by Floyd Bland, all rights reserved. No part of this book may be reproduced, transmitted, or stored except as provided under U.S. copyright laws.

This book is for Christian inspirational purposes and does not replace the advice or services of qualified clinical or legal professionals.

At press time, the author and publisher attempted to provide accurate subject content. Neither the publisher nor author assumes any liability for loss or damage caused by content errors or omissions.

The scenarios and fictional stories are imaginary. The author has also altered persons or events for anonymity. Any similarity to actual persons, living or dead, entities, or locales is coincidental.

Scripture quotations are from the Authorized (King James) Version (AKJV). Rights in the Authorized Version in the United Kingdom are vested in the Crown. Reproduced by permission of the Crown's patentee, Cambridge University Press.

ISBN Number: 978-1-7325342-5-4
Library of Congress Control Number: 2022901316

For those who love His appearing

Contents

Preface: Why I Believe in the Christian Heritage   viii
    My Story, Living Proof, Changing the World

With Gratitude   xv

Introduction: Called to Glory and Virtue   1
    A Sin Problem, God's Intervention: Jesus Christ

Chapter One: Diligently Add to Your Faith   13
    What is Faith?, The Object of Faith: Jesus Christ, The
    Result of Faith and Repentance

Chapter Two: Add Virtue to Your Faith   27
    Not for Men Only, Personal Virtue, Social Virtue, God's
    People Act Differently, A Problem with Money

Chapter Three: Add Knowledge to Your Virtue   38
    The Reverend Dr. L. B. Moss, What is Knowledge?, Our
    Need for Christian Discipleship, Christian Service, The
    Importance of Christian Experience, Double Trouble

Chapter Four: Add Temperance to Your Knowledge   51
    Temperance vs. Self-Indulgence, My Observation, What's
    It Worth?

Chapter Five: Add Patience to Your Temperance   63
    Who Shall Endure?, God's Providence and Preservation,
    A Persevering Attachment to Christ, A Missionary, a
    Preacher, and an Old Man

Chapter Six: Add Godliness to Your Patience   76
    God's Holiness and Our Godliness, Godliness Revealed,
    For the Sake of the Call

Chapter Seven: Add Brotherly Kindness to Your Godliness   84
    From Partiality to Family, We Are a Christian Family, A
    True Friend

Chapter Eight: Add Love to Your Brotherly Kindness   95
    A New Commandment, God's Love Becomes Human,
    The Greatest of These is Love, Abiding in Love

Epilogue: Not I, But Christ   104
    One Saturday, Over the Years, The Next Step

Appendices
    Appendix A: Suggested Christian Heritage Code   110
    Appendix B: Suggested Scenario Answers   111

About the Author   113

Preface
Why I Believe in the Christian Heritage

My Story

When giving testimony, many can tell the precise day they accepted Jesus Christ as Lord and Savior. I can't, because I came to know Him early, and living for Him has since consumed me. This was not my doing, as the Lord gave me wonderful parents and guardians who showed their love for me by introducing me to Jesus Christ early in life. Then, they showed their love for God through consistent, Christ-centered behavior.

Unlike today, where selfish indifference and isolation are the norm, I can remember a time when there were many strong, God-fearing, Christian "surrogate" parents. They were my extended family, who offered my contemporaries and me the care, guidance, advice, and discipline we needed to grow into God-fearing, responsible, and productive adults.

The Lord placed me in a spiritually nurturing environment, where I learned fundamental biblical principles that still inform my faith and conduct today. I yet admire those dedicated men and women who showed a sacred, reverential fear for God and His Word, coupled with an urgency for the Lord's imminent return, as did Job,

> For I know that my redeemer liveth, and that he shall stand at the latter day upon the earth: And though after my skin worms destroy this body, yet in my flesh shall I see God: Whom I

shall see for myself, and mine eyes shall behold, and not another; though my reins be consumed within me. (Job 19:25–27)

I cannot overstate the importance of having my father, mother, and grandmother, along with "surrogate" caregivers, to model Christ-centered living during my formative years. What I learned from the Lord and the Bible, connected with what I gleaned from watching and emulating them, helped me to navigate the "straight and narrow" path I've since trodden.

It further rescued me from the myriad of "voices" that beckoned so many of us during that turbulent era of the '60s. The Space Race, Vietnam, the Beatles, Motown, James Brown, Jimi Hendrix, Civil Rights, the Black Panthers, the Hippies, the Nation of Islam, Berkeley, Woodstock, Haight-Ashbury, "We Shall Overcome," "What the World Needs Now is Love," "Say It Loud," "My Sweet Lord," "Day By Day," "Aquarius/Let the Sunshine In," "Burn Baby, Burn," "Turn On," "Tune In," "Drop Out," "Sit In," "Love In," and "God Is Dead." These distinct voices, and the tragic deaths of JFK, Malcolm, Martin, Bobby, and others, demanded our nation's undivided attention, as well as its underserved people—especially this poor black kid from the projects.

Amidst the chaos, Jesus' gentle whisper invited me to trust Him with my heart, and not rely on my understanding; to acknowledge Him in all my ways, so that He can direct my paths, as Proverbs 3:5–6 contends.

I may have grown spiritually, but I've not arrived at completion. Sometimes I do not model our Lord's spiritual and moral excellence. However, I strive for completion in Him each day. My way of life has not been the proverbial "bed of roses." Still, I yearn for the abundant life He desires for all those who seek Him.

During each trial, He has provided the joy, peace, and means to overcome it in a manner whereby He receives the glory. Since no words can express my thanks for His faithfulness and mercy over the years, I strive to please Him forever.

"Living Proof"

To refute the notion that Jesus Christ was both God and man, naysayers argue that relying on Christ alone to redeem us is futile, and we need more than a "dead" prophet to save us. My response is in a paraphrase 2 Timothy 1:12, "I know in whom I believe, and I am fully persuaded that He is more than able to keep everything I've entrusted to Him forever."

I've committed my life to the Lord because He is not one of many ways to God. He is the only way,

> I am the way, the truth, and the life: no man cometh unto the Father, but by me. (John 14:6)

As Son of God (God) and Son of Man (human), Jesus Christ is the only person in history who could make these bold assertions. He insists Abraham rejoiced to see His day, and that before Abraham was I AM. Such an unprecedented link with Israel's Old Testament Covenant God (YHWH) was blasphemy—punishable with death. (John 8:56-59)

He was the Seed of the Woman promised to Abraham, through whom the entire human race benefits. (Genesis 3:15; 12:1–3) He was God's Suffering Servant who redeemed a lost humanity, as Isaiah foretells,

> All we like sheep have gone astray; we have turned every one to his own way; and the LORD hath laid on him the iniquity of us all. (Isaiah 53:6)

As the Good Shepherd, His vicarious death imparts new life to His precious sheep just as He promises,

> The Thief [Satan] cometh not, but for to steal, and to kill, and to destroy: I am come that they might have life, and that they might have it more abundantly. (John 10:10)

Our Lord's mission and message was about the Kingdom of God (or Heaven). It was distinct from anything the world had witnessed before, and His theme was simple,

> Verily, verily, I say unto thee, Except a man be born again, he cannot see the kingdom of God. (John 3:3)

Further,

> Thou shalt love the Lord thy God with all thy heart, and with all thy soul, and with all thy mind. This is the first and great commandment. And the second is like unto it, Thou shalt love thy neighbour as thyself. (Matthew 22:37-40)

Peter expounded on these profound ideals when he answered his naysayers,

> For there is none other name under heaven given among men, whereby we must be saved. (Acts 4:12)

Jesus Christ, who died for our sins and rose for our justification, offers us absolute, eternal safekeeping. (Romans 4:25) *Amen!*

I wrote this book to show how Christians are the "living proof" of God's marvelous redemptive plan. I chose the title, *The Christian Heritage*, because we are the joint heirs to whom Jesus entrusts the *New Birth*.

The Christian Heritage is the new life we share in common through Christ, as He reigns as Savior, Lord, and Benefactor. His priceless heirloom confirms our identity as followers of Christ who live morally responsible and spiritually astute lives that enhance and preserve a civil society.

Changing the World

It's God's perfect desire that we participate in His grace and love, as John writes,

> But as many as received him, to them gave he power to become the sons of God, even to them that believe on his name: Which were born, not of blood, nor of the will of the flesh, nor of the will of man, but of God. (John 1:12–13)

I believe in the Christian heritage, and I've spent a lifetime helping others realize it as well. We are neither "barren nor unfruitful" as we walk in the knowledge of our Lord Jesus Christ. Human lives change in the presence of the Living Christ, and changed lives (Christ-centered and Spirit-controlled) think, speak, and act in ways that are not detrimental to the health, welfare, or safety of other people regardless of race, gender, culture, social status, or political affiliation.

It is possible to change the world—one person at a time. Before presenting *The Christian Heritage*, I will share the words of an old hymn that encapsulates my journey.

The Old Rugged Cross[1]
George Bennard (1873–1958)

On a hill far away stood an old rugged cross,

---

[1] George Bennard, "The Old Rugged Cross," *101 Hymn Stories*, Kenneth W. Osbeck, (Grand Rapids: Kregel Publications, 1982), 254.

The emblem of suffering and shame;
And I love that old cross where the dearest and best For a world of lost sinners was slain.

O that old rugged cross, so despised by the world, Has a wondrous attraction for me;
For the dear Lamb of God left His glory above, To bear it to dark Calvary.

In the old rugged cross, stained with blood so divine, A wondrous beauty I see;
For 'twas on that old cross Jesus suffered and died, To pardon and sanctify me.

To the old rugged cross I will ever be true,
Its shame and reproach gladly bear;
Then He'll call me some day to my home far away, Where His glory forever I'll share.

Chorus:
So Ill cherish the old rugged cross,
Till my trophies at last I lay down;
I will cling to the old rugged cross,
And exchange it some day for a crown.

With Gratitude

I thank God for sending His Son to die for me and for sealing me with His Spirit until He comes for me along with all those who love His appearing. (2 Timothy 4:8)

I thank God for my parents and immediate family for your love, faith, commitment to Christ, support, and encouragement these many years.

To those unsung heroes and heroines, whose prayers, help, inspiration, lifestyle, and instruction helped me along my life's journey, thank you.

To Suzanne Robitaille of Second Look Editorial Services and Paramita Bhattacharjee of Creative Paramita Book Cover Designs, I am grateful to God for your professionalism and expertise rendered to prepare this book for publication.

Introduction
Called to Glory and Virtue

The heart is deceitful above all things, and desperately wicked: who can know it? (Jeremiah 17:9)

A Sin Problem

Imagine living where pain, sadness, and illness do not exist, where the fulfillment of your desires, wishes, and aspirations occurs daily. In this perfect environment of innocence, tranquility, and serenity, you flourish with your loved ones.

Impossible? Not so, because God created Adam and Eve, and He placed them in the Garden of Eden with everything they needed—or desired. Eternal bliss was theirs as long as they obeyed God: "You must not eat from the tree of the knowledge of good and evil; for in the day that you eat of it, you will surely die." (Genesis 2:17)

The moment they ate the fruit, death occurred instantly. Although their physical deaths would manifest over time, their spiritual death (the Fall) was immediate, contaminating the world with sin. (Genesis 2:16–17; 3:6–19, Romans 5:12)

Thus, we have a sinful condition (Fallen Nature or Nature) that influences how we interact with each other, such that toddlers can combat their parents, teenagers can conduct brutal murders, and adults do other heinous acts that cause us to wonder how civilized human beings could commit such atrocities.

A recent pandemic hysteria has influenced far too many of us to an extent that I find baffling. I can remember when our society (and our rule of law) preserved the distinct contrast between right and wrong.

Our society widely respected and welcomed prayer, the Ten Commandments, and Judeo-Christian values in our public discourse. Now, we vilify the righteous and praise the wicked to our own peril, just as the Bible warns,

> Righteousness exalteth a nation: but sin is a reproach to any people. (Proverbs 14:34)

Further,

> Woe unto them that call evil good, and good evil; that put darkness for light, and light for darkness; that put bitter for sweet, and sweet for bitter. (Isaiah 5:20)

Although sin's tragic effects surround us daily, as witnessed in our selfishness, lust, greed, hatred, violence, pride, exploitation, and many other forms of consistent destructive behavior, still we resort to denial in our attempt to eliminate its existence.

Someone who lives a "decent life" will contend, "I can't be a sinner. I do good deeds!" Similarly, denying the existence of gravity does not make it so either. "I can't see, hear, taste, touch, or smell it," someone might say. However, they will have a rude awakening when they step off a ledge that is a thousand feet in the air without safety netting or precautions underneath them.

People who deny being sinners don't realize that our sinful behavior does not make us so. We are sinners because of our inherited sin nature, constantly working in us, and we need God's safety netting to rescue us from peril.

I have worked with those who've faced strong public resistance after completing their prison sentences. Perhaps the community fears they will vandalize property, steal valuables, assault friends or family members, or commit a dangerous act. If we can be finicky about our associations, should we not expect a holy God to be selective with whom He spends eternity? God did not fall from perfection. We did, and our *Fallen Nature* offends Him, and violates His "no riffraff allowed" policy.

One way we try to earn God's favor is by keeping the Law. God gave us the Old Testament Law (Law) through Moses to define sin and righteousness from His perspective. With this irrefutable record, we have His promise of peace and prosperity. It defines our proper worship, service, and love and remains applicable today as the Lord promises,

> Till heaven and earth pass, one jot or one tittle shall in no wise pass from the Law, till all be fulfilled. (Matthew 5:18b)

God's righteousness should be attainable when we keep the Law, right? But we worship other gods, create idols, irreverently use the Lord's name, break the Sabbath, disrespect our parents, commit murder, are sexually promiscuous, steal, lie, and covet. If Ten Commandments are difficult, imagine how impossible 613 statutes of the Old Testament Law would be. The Law makes no one righteous. It only serves to remind us how condemned we are—because we can't keep it!

Another way we try to please God is through enterprise and accomplishment. Yet, nothing we do can correct a sin-skewed inner nature. Daily, we see the tragic futility of people seeking remedies through wealth, sporting accomplishments and notoriety, political power, entertainment, corporate advancement, social status, academia, technology, science, and medicine. Our failures show we are morally and spiritually bankrupt, unfit to access a glorious Heaven. Yet, they suit us perfectly for occupying a tormenting Hell forever.

Other flawed approaches are self-righteous denial, self-determination, and/or self-will. Proudly and defiantly refusing to acknowledge our sin, as if it does not exist, or self-willing to be "better" through sheer determination, is comparable to

Adam and Eve using fig leaves to mask their guilt and nakedness, which didn't work.

Our ancestors' guilt and shame prevented them from facing the Lord when He approached them. Gone was the sincere, honest, uncorrupted intimacy with God. The new norm would to hide, lie, and blame to conceal disobedience and sin. We've not changed our tactics as we still resort to cover-up, rationalizing, and fault finding to escape personal accountability.

Human effort will not change our nature. Spiritually separated from God, we cannot have fellowship with Him until we have the clean hands and pure hearts He requires,

> Who shall ascend into the hill of the LORD? or who shall stand in his holy place? He that hath clean hands, and a pure heart; who hath not lifted up his soul unto vanity, nor sworn deceitfully. He shall receive the blessing from the LORD, and righteousness from the God of his salvation. (Psalm 24:3–5)

God hints to a better remedy for sin in Leviticus 17:11,

> For the life of the flesh is in the blood: and I have given it to you upon the altar to make an atonement for your souls: for it is the blood that maketh an atonement for the soul.

God gave Moses specific instructions for erecting an altar to use "clean" animals (e.g., sheep, goats, bulls, etc.) to cover our sin. Yet, animal sacrifices did not solve the sin problem. They merely foreshadowed a more effective remedy through a Redeemer who would blot out sin, make us righteous, and restore our eternal fellowship forever.

God's Intervention: Jesus Christ
God could have solved our sin problem by programming us to obey Him like robots. But He wanted us to love Him freely and surrender to Him willingly. He could have created loopholes and exemptions in the Law to accommodate our sin; but sacrificing His perfection for our imperfection would make Him less than holy. He chose the most effective remedy instead by becoming a human being (*The Incarnation*) in the person of Jesus Christ so that He could pay the price for our sin Himself,

> And the Word was made flesh, and dwelt among us, and we beheld his glory, the glory as of the only begotten of the Father, full of grace and truth. (John 1:14)

At the onset of His earthly ministry, Jesus Christ announced He could resolve our sin problem with His sinless life and precious blood when He declared,

> The time is fulfilled, and the kingdom of God is at hand: repent ye, and believe the gospel. (Mark 1:15)

His was the greatest proclamation in history because it heralded a New Testament age for all people everywhere. We have our sins forgiven, experience a complete, internal, spiritual transformation, and we can have our intimacy with God restored, as Hebrews 9:11-12 states,

> But Christ being come an high priest of good things to come, by a greater and more perfect tabernacle, not made with hands, that is to say, not of this building; Neither by the blood of goats and calves, but by his own blood he entered in once into the holy place, having obtained eternal redemption for us.

This new period in history also revoked all claims of neutrality toward God. In John 8:24, Jesus warns how those who reject Him will die in their sins. Either we can choose to receive His gift of abundant life on earth and eternal life in Heaven, or we can reject Him and face an empty, unfulfilled life on earth and a tormented eternity in Hell.

Of Jesus' Disciples, Judas was the one who was so preoccupied with acquiring a worldly kingdom that he rejected the Lord and forever changed His identity from Disciple to traitor with a single kiss.

Thirty pieces of silver were too much to resist, and without Christ as Redeemer, Hell awaited him.

Jesus knew Judas was a godless degenerate, yet He chose him to be one of the Twelve. How the Lord loved him and gave him every opportunity to repent. Three years, He presented His redemptive plan to Judas through moral and spiritual excellence, astonishing miracles, and eternal truths,

> Enter ye in at the strait gate: for wide is the gate, and broad is the way, that leadeth to destruction, and many there be which go in thereat: Because strait is the gate, and narrow is the way, which leadeth unto life, and few there be that find it. (Matthew 7:13–14)

Judas' example provides hope for everyone, especially those feeling God has forgotten them or that they are beyond His redemption. Judas shows us how patient, gracious, and loving the Lord is. He extends Himself to the worst of us, willing to give rest to those who labor under heavy loads, with a yoke that is easy and a burden that is light. (Matthew 11:30) *What a wonderful Savior!*

Simon, another Disciple, recognized and understood the importance of having a sincere, penitent, and reverent faith in Christ. The Lord saw this impetuous, rock-solid leader and changed his name to Peter, or the Greek *petros* (Strong-G4074), meaning "rock." Jesus warned

Simon that Satan would sift him as wheat. (Luke 22:31-32) Although he denied the Lord three times, he repented and later became the leader of the Apostles. As Peter, the Rock, he fed his Lord's precious sheep and helped the New Testament Church flourish during its infancy. In his Second Epistle, he articulates the church's mission and message,

> And beside this, giving all diligence, add to your faith virtue; and to virtue knowledge; and to knowledge temperance; and to temperance patience; and to patience godliness; and to godliness brotherly kindness; and to brotherly kindness charity [love]. For if these things be in you, and abound, they make you that ye shall neither be barren nor unfruitful in the knowledge of our Lord Jesus Christ. (2 Peter 1:5–8)

Peter implies the Lord possessed eight moral/spiritual attributes that His followers (Believers) emulate. As the living stones being built into a spiritual house for His glory (1 Peter 2:5), we fulfill His promise that we are "not of the world" and are recipients of God's transforming grace. (John 15:19; 17:14, 16) Only God can transform vile sinners into His holy people as the Protestant Reformer, Martin Luther observes,

> Now there are many peoples in the world; the Christians, however, are a people with a special call and are therefore called not

> just ecclesia, 'church,' or, 'people,' but sancta catholica Christiana, that is, 'a Christian holy people' who believe in Christ. That is why they are called a Christian people and have the Holy Spirit, who sanctifies them daily. [2]

We serve with humility and gratitude for what the Lord did for us, that we were unwilling and incapable. We refrain from pride, sin, and selfishness to practice humility, righteousness, and generosity. As His salt and light (Matthew 5:13-14), we depict His noble character. Anything less (or living like the world) is comparable to worthless, tasteless salt.

We grow more like Christ daily, and we honor Him by our character and conduct. Our new Spirit-driven life is born out of a sincere faith, which gives us the clean hands and pure hearts that God requires. Our spiritual transformation affirms the Word of God,

> I am crucified with Christ: nevertheless I live; yet not I, but Christ liveth in me: and the life which I now live in the flesh I live by the faith of the Son of God, who loved me, and gave himself for me. (Galatians 2:20)

---

[2] Timothy F. Lull, ed., *Martin Luther's Basic Theological Teachings* (Minneapolis: Fortress Press, 1989), 540.

Over time, the power of Satan, the cares of this world, and our own human frailties no longer debilitate us as we function under His unfaltering might. Are we perfect? No, but God is! He provides the spiritual strength we need while we await His glorious Heaven.

Through faith, virtue, knowledge, temperance, patience, godliness, brotherly kindness, and love, the Lord can use us to answer complex questions and solve troublesome problems that constantly baffle our spiritually lost, morally decadent, and ever-yearning world.

This book outlines eight moral/spiritual attributes through supporting scriptures, works of other authors, interactive illustrations, and provocative scenarios. In Chapter One, we explore the spiritual operations of faith. The Appendices feature a Suggested Christian Heritage Code and Suggested Answers to the Scenarios. I will present theological terms in italics for further research throughout the book as well. I pray the Lord uses this book to strengthen your faith, so that He receives the honor as we benefit collectively.

Christ is returning for His bride, a glorious church filled with simple, ordinary people who have neither spots nor blemishes—no exceptions. Will you be ready?

Faith

Chapter One
Diligently Add to Your Faith

What is Faith?
The Greek word for Faith is *pistis* (Strong-G4102), which describes our trust in someone or something to accomplish a task that is beyond our current level of understanding. A father asked Jesus to heal his boy, whose violent seizures and inability to talk threatened his safety. The Lord told the boy's father that faith makes everything, including his child's recovery, possible.

Fear and anxiety hit the father because his son's condition was his present "reality." For healing to occur, he could no longer rely on his senses. He needed a "leap of faith," by relying on what he could not prove scientifically or explain logically.

The father placed his faith in what he could not see, feel, touch, taste, or smell because he wanted his child restored. Thus, he replied most reverently, "Lord, I believe; help thou mine unbelief." (Mark 9:24b) That day, Jesus healed both the son and father.

We must blend the "cold, hard facts of life" with the transcendent and eternal—often inexplicable—for faith to occur. Otherwise, we adopt flawed faith concepts. Some of us view faith as an instrument to impose our will on God. We see God not as the almighty and all-knowing Creator and Sustainer. Instead, He is our puppet-genie to do our bidding whenever we "pull His strings."

Nevertheless, God does what suits Him, in His precise manner, at His precise moment. His ways may appear mysterious. Yet, they are invariably perfect because He knows what is best for us.

Convinced God does not exist, and things are haphazard, some of us see faith as aimless wishing. Yet, faith is part of our daily, material lives. Without it, we would scrutinize our air, water, food, furniture, electrical appliances, motor vehicles, boats, airplanes—anything we planned to use before using it. At all the airports I've visited, I've yet to see passengers insist on seeing the pilot's credentials at the ticket counter. We have faith the airlines select qualified pilots to fly the planes.

Another flawed view links our faith with feelings. Here, our faith is stable when we feel good. Yet, the *Enemy* (*Satan*), our pride, selfishness, emotional wounds, cravings, and well-meaning people can influence our feelings and deceive us.

Our faith should be in God, who is faithful to us, regardless of how we feel. Job cursed the day of his birth, yet, he maintained faith in God. Paul spoke of how we should not have faith in visible and temporary, but in the invisible and eternal. Jesus says we can move mountains with "mustard seed" faith. Feelings should have no bearing on our faith's quantity or fervor.

Faith is a mystery that is essential to our relationship with God. Abraham was seventy-five when God commanded him to go to an unspecified location. He obeyed without wavering because he sought to live in a land where God was the master architect.

Such conviction in the face of tremendous uncertainty was unprecedented. No one before Abraham showed a willingness to obey God with such unrealized trust,

> He was a person of great sagacity...; for he was the first that ventured to publish the notion that there was but one God, the Creator of the universe; and that, as to the other [gods], if they contributed anything to the happiness of men, that each of them afforded it only according to his appointment, and not by their own power.[3]

Taking his wife and nephew with him, Abraham depended on the unseen for his survival, and God rewarded him with a solemn promise,

> And I will bless them that bless thee, and curse him that curseth thee: and in thee shall all families of the earth be blessed. (Genesis 12:3)

---

[3] Flavius Josephus, "Josephus Complete Works," *The Antiquities of the Jews*, Book I, Chapter vii, trans. William Whiston, reprint (Grand Rapids: Kregel Publications, 1978), 32.

We honor Abraham for spawning a nation, and a faith movement that's still vibrant today.

Others in the Bible noted for their faith include Noah, whose ark saved humanity from the flood; Joseph, whose false imprisonment saved his nation; Ruth, whose lineage would include David and Jesus Christ, David, who defeated Goliath and delivered God's chosen people from a fierce enemy.

Isaiah pondered the elusiveness of redeeming faith when he asked,

> Who hath believed our report? and to whom is the arm of the LORD revealed? (Isaiah 53:1)

This age-old question presents a passive and active faith with one object: Jesus Christ.

The Object of Faith: Jesus Christ
As the Son of God, Jesus was 100 percent God. He showed an imposing mastery over His creation that verified His claims to be the Son of God. He commanded the elements, calmed the turbulent sea, walked on water, turned water into wine, multiplied two fish and five loaves to feed the enormous crowd, healed the sick, and raised the dead.

In addition, Jesus was completely human as well. As the Son of Man, He shared our wants, needs, and desires. He felt hunger, thirst, fatigue, sorrow, anger, and loneliness. He also had aspirations and felt temptation. The difference is that He maintained a balanced life of moral and spiritual excellence. He did not succumb to the lusts of the flesh or selfish motives, but submitted to the will of His Father to satisfy the Law. *He was perfect!*

In the Introduction, we explored how our Nature separates us from God, who now solves our sin problem by drawing us to Christ (passive) so that we can have faith in Him (active). Through our repentance and faith, the Lord restores our eternal fellowship, and gives us peace and favor with God.

The Results of Faith and Repentance

Although consuming and tantalizing, sin does not fulfill our deep longings as does a personal relationship with the Lord Jesus Christ, and we cannot have this relationship when we are pursuing a life of sin. Faith leads to repentance. Beyond just a historical figure, Jesus Christ becomes real and personal,

> We believe the Scriptures teach that repentance and faith are sacred duties and also inseparable graces, wrought in the soul by the regenerating Spirit of God; whereby being deeply convinced of our guilt, danger, and helplessness, and of the way of salvation by Christ, we turn to God with unfeigned contrition, confession, and supplication for mercy; at the same time heartily receiving the Lord Jesus as our

prophet, priest, and king, and relying on Him alone as the only and all-sufficient Savior.[4]

Blood sustains human life, and God uses it to remediate sin. (Leviticus 17:11 and Hebrews 9:22) A sinless Jesus Christ shed His blood to pay sin's price—past, present, and future.

Consciously, deliberately, and reverently, we admit our sin offends God, and that Christ's sacrificial death supersedes our best efforts. We repent (or change our minds) about pursuing our former life of sin and turn to Christ, inviting Him to be our personal Lord and Savior.

God changes us forever to pursue Christ and His righteousness, completely released from sin's domination as promised in Ezekiel 36:25–27,

> Then will I sprinkle clean water upon you, and ye shall be clean: from all your filthiness, and from all your idols, will I cleanse you. A new heart also will I give you, and a new spirit will I put within you: and I will take away the stony heart out of your flesh, and I will give you an heart of flesh. And I will put my spirit within you, and cause you to walk in my

---

[4] Edward T. Hiscox, *The Standard Manual for Baptist Churches* (Philadelphia: The American Baptist Publication Society, 1951), 64.

statutes, and ye shall keep my judgments, and do them.

The Lord changes our being, position, choices, and destiny through four spiritual operations.

> *The First Spiritual Operation: Changing Our Nature*

God eliminates our Nature forever by the *New Birth*.[5] Jesus describes this transformation as a prerequisite for fellowship with God by faith. (John 3:3–8) As dying people lived because they believed Moses' snake would save them, Jesus said we could live forever by trusting in the redemptive act He will perform at Calvary,

> And as Moses lifted up the serpent in the wilderness, even so must the Son of man be lifted up: That whosoever believeth in him should not perish, but have eternal life. For God so loved the world, that he gave his only begotten Son, that whosoever believeth in him should not perish, but have everlasting life. For God sent not his Son into the world to condemn the world; but that the world

---

[5] "*New Birth*," "*In Christ*," "*Born Again*," and "*Union with Christ*" are synonymous terms that refer to our spiritual collaboration with God, whereby we reach to Christ with repentance and faith (*Conversion*), and God's Holy Spirit *Quickens* us (*Regeneration*).

through him might be saved. (John 3:14–17)

Through our humble submission, God transforms us so that we can perform His will, secure His favor, and become His beloved children. No longer spiritually dead and sin tarnished, we are alive and invigorated. As sunlight obliterates the darkness, God's Spirit obliterates our dark bondage to sin.

Some people associate the New Birth with materialism. Still, this is not the case since God's Kingdom is spiritual, not material. We yearn for power, influence, and dominance while He desires our transformed hearts. Thus, we may not have our names listed in *Who's Who,* or gain wealth, influence, or notoriety. Yet, we have a new, internal spiritual being that makes us acceptable before God,

> Regeneration involves the illumination of the understanding, the consecration of the affections, and the rectification of the will. To use Paul's language, 'Ye were once darkness, but now are ye light in the Lord,' Ephesians v. 8. [6]

Truly, we are new creatures in Christ!

---

[6] J. M. Pendleton, *Christian Doctrines*, 33rd printing (Valley Forge: Judson Press, 1976), 59.

> *The Second Spiritual Operation: God Declares Us Righteous*

By faith, God gives us a new standing before Him by replacing our sinful life with Jesus' sinless life, making us righteous forever (*Justification*). Through Christ, we fulfill God's Law and become suitable for His eternal fellowship,

> But he was wounded for our transgressions, he was bruised for our iniquities: the chastisement of our peace was upon him; and with his stripes we are healed. (Isaiah 53:5)

We stood before God, condemned for our Nature and sin. Yet, Jesus takes on our sin, guilt, and penalty and gives us His innocence, righteousness, and glory. We now have a new identity: righteousness, with an expunged sinful history. It's not our works, but faith in *His works* that secure our eternal destiny.

Jesus Christ loves us more than we could ever comprehend. Romans Chapter 5 outlines how sin separates us from God, but His precious blood reconciles us. We are at peace with God, and no longer enemies. This is God's grace, and it's amazing.

> *The Third Spiritual Operation: We Are Under the Holy Spirit's Influence*

The Holy Spirit produces good fruit and molds us into Jesus' likeness (*Sanctification*), as Jesus foretells,

> Ye are the light of the world. A city that is set on an hill cannot be hid. Neither do men light a candle, and put it under a bushel, but on a candlestick; and it giveth light unto all that are in the house. Let your light so shine before men, that they may see your good works, and glorify your Father which is in heaven. Matthew 5:14–16)

Romans 12:2 states,

> And be not conformed to this world: but be ye transformed by the renewing of your mind, that ye may prove what is that good, and acceptable, and perfect, will of God.

A renewed mind produces a growing disdain for the worldly things, which hinder our moral and spiritual growth. It also produces a progressive yearning for godly things like reading His Word, prayer, worship, Christian fellowship, and service.

We collaborate with the Lord in His spiritual operation to make godly, moral choices deliberately while performing selfless acts intentionally,

> That in this conflict the Holy Spirit enables the Christian, through increasing faith, more fully and consciously to appropriate Christ, and thus progressively to make

conquest of the remaining sinfulness of his nature.[7]

Although we surrender the control of our lives to the Lord each day, we will not achieve perfection. (If this were possible, there would be no need for Christ to die for sin. We'd be perfect without him.)

We grieve the Holy Spirit by walking in sin instead of walking in the Spirit. Then, like the Prodigal Son (Luke 15:11–32), we "come to ourselves" and return to the Lord, so He can strengthen our ability to conduct ourselves nobly and make sound decisions.

Our imperfection does not dissuade our fervor for Christ. It reminds us how far we are from His perfection and teaches us to rely on His strength daily. Our perfection in Christ produces an honorable lifestyle to contrast our former life of sin.

The Fourth Spiritual Operation: On to Our Final Destination

The Bible teaches that flesh and blood cannot inherit the Kingdom of God. (1 Corinthians 15:50) When our Lord calls us from labor to reward, we will experience the pinnacle of His redemptive work where the wicked cease from troubling and

---

[7] Agustus H. Strong, *Systematic Theology*, 31st printing (Valley Forge: Judson Press, 1976), 870.

the weary are at rest. (Job 3:17) Of this glorious transformation, the Scriptures attest,

> So when this corruptible shall have put on incorruption, and this mortal shall have put on immortality, then shall be brought to pass the saying that is written, death is swallowed up in victory. (1 Corinthians 15:54)

This is our present hope and eternal destiny (*Glorification*). God will give us immortal bodies that will resemble Christ's resurrected body. Then we can fully experience God's magnificent presence, free from sin, pain, and disease. We will see Him "as He is" and be like Him. (1 John 3:2)

Far too many people live for the here and now: *"three-score and ten, and the most toys win!"* Howbeit, there is a vast eternity beyond the grave, and we must acknowledge Jesus Christ is Lord and Savior in this life to avoid eternal peril,

> For what is a man profited, if he shall gain the whole world, and lose his own soul? or what shall a man give in exchange for his soul? (Matthew 16:26)

Proud, self-righteous human endeavors will never invoke God's favor, as does Calvary's Cross. It's never been about us; it's about Jesus Christ, and our faith in Him vitalizes our being, position, conduct, and eternal destiny.

Those who don't acknowledge Him now will face Him as Eternal Judge then. However, we who love Him, and whose faith begins and ends with Him, He is our hope, peace, expectation, and glorious reward. Galatians 3:11 reads, "The just shall live by faith," and 2 Corinthians 5:7 states, "We walk by faith, not by sight." James 4:6 tells us that God resists the proud and gives grace to the humble—*does He ever!*

Like airplanes on a runway before takeoff, we cannot fly without our Eternal Pilot at the controls. With humble, reverent, and sincere faith in Him, we shall reach our glorious final destination safely.

In this chapter, we explored faith. We'll look at virtue in the next.

Virtue

Chapter Two
Add Virtue to Your Faith

Not for Men Only

Our society has bought into many "manhood" stereotypes to attain the "perfect" design for human interpersonal relationships. We "take it like a man," and put on facades to cover our weakness. As "masters of our destiny," we do what is in our "best interests." Even so, our methods to achieve these ends often imperil another person's physical, financial, or emotional well-being.

Men aren't alone. Women and children are culpable in chasing "the good life." We expect people to have a "me-first" agenda, where abusing, exploiting, or traumatizing people is commonplace. For ours is a "dog-eat-dog world" where "only the strong survive," where the "ends justify the means," because "it's not personal; it's only business." So obsessed is our society, which once advocated honesty and integrity, that now even professing Christians resort to duplicity to "get paid," and like a troubled sea, there is neither rest nor peace. (Isaiah 57:20–21)

Our modern world might discredit moral strength, but God doesn't. His eternal purpose is to create offspring who will do justly, love mercy, and walk humbly each day. Jesus declared those who follow Him would have the light of life, affirming His righteousness and ours. (Micah 6:8, John 8:12)

Physical exertion does not measure our strength. As the Lord showed, respectable moral conduct is a wonderful example of human strength in character. Consistent with His example, we add virtue; or the Greek *arete* (Strong-G703), or noble behavior to our faith. Jesus is The Vine, and we are His branches, who yield bountiful produce,

> "I am the vine, ye are the branches: He that abideth in me, and I in him, the same bringeth forth much fruit: for without me ye can do nothing." (John 15:5)

Virtue, our captivating personal and social witness, contrasts the societal pretense and dishonesty we find so commonplace today.

Personal Virtue
We are not sanctimonious exhibitionists who seek to impress with self-righteous piety. We covenant with the Lord humbly and reverently. His Spirit gives us the moral strength to make sure the "who we are when no one is watching" acts appropriately.

Without Jesus, we were villainous. With Him, we are virtuous. He replaces our deceit with sincerity, and our duplicity with integrity. We keep our word and tell the truth in love.

When temptation leads to sin, we do not mask our immorality with blame and excuses. We ask the Lord and the offended person for forgiveness; we reconcile with the aggrieved, and we choose not to repeat the transgression. Seeking counsel from pastors, qualified professionals, or entrusted Christian friends can help us stay the course toward health and healing. [8]

As did Jesus, we grow in wisdom, stature, and favor with God and humanity. (Luke 2:52) Another's ability and accomplishments do not threaten or intimidate us. Emotionally secure, we refrain from jealousy and envy. We know the Lord makes people rise and fall, and we trust in His infinite wisdom and providence. We are not proud or boastful about our status or possessions. As God's stewards, He blesses us to help people in need, and He commands our faithfulness.

Personal virtue allows us to protect, preserve, and strengthen our bodies through rest, exercise, and diet. We avoid unhealthy stress and abstain from drug or alcohol abuse. We are a positive witness to others when we take part in sporting events, as good winners or losers, because He's at the center. Not passive about spiritual maturity, we seek to outgrow tendencies toward sin, Satan, and self. We fast, pray, read/study God's Word, attend church, and serve others while striving for home and church environments that are wholesome.

---

[8] For recovery from a traumatic episode or compulsive-addictive behavior, seeking help from a qualified professional is highly recommended.

Home

God established the home as the place where we create caring relations. As precious cargo, we pray and play together as unique individuals of one homogeneous unit. Everyone is safe from sexual, physical, and emotional abuse, as we treat each other with dignity and respect—not gratification instruments. Comforting words that nurture and support replace cutting and insulting talk.

Using Christ's unselfish affection as a model, husbands love their spouses to the point of dying for them. Cherished wives share in the responsibilities of maintaining the Christ-centered home where parents/guardians and children have well-defined roles. Parents/guardians raise, train, protect and give care for their children, while kids accept their caregiver's guidance unless caregiver abuse is present. [9]

Parents refrain from cynicism, hostility, and condemnation to give love, support, and affirmation, while modeling sincerity, truth, and reliability. Caregivers administer consistent and proper discipline to encourage kids to be accountable. Not provoking children to anger, caregivers help kids understand the consequences of poor choices and wrong behavior. This will help them become safe, respectful, and sociable members of civil society.

---

[9] Local municipalities have reporting guidelines for abuse that are to be followed.

Parents expose, train, and advocate Christian values to kids while they are young. (Proverbs 22:6, Ecclesiastes 12:1) This helps youngsters develop constructive, godly pursuits instead of destructive, worldly ones. Kids can devote themselves to the Lord as they engage secular or religious vocations for life.

Jesus teaches us in Matthew 5:45 that God allows the "sun to shine" and the "rain to fall" on the "just and unjust" indiscriminately. Thus, families are not exempt from life's vicissitudes, yet, we trust the Lord through our trials and adversity. There may be times when the parent/guardian becomes incapacitated and the children take on the responsibility to provide "parental" care for them. When children serve in this manner, they not only express their love and appreciation for their parent/guardian tangibly and meaningfully. They also fulfill God's command to honor their parents/guardians as Exodus 2:12 teaches.

> *Church*

The church is where God's people gather to worship, honor, and serve Him faithfully. Here, we fellowship, serve, and observe our Lord's ordinances. Pastors and leaders help us grow by giving care and instruction, promoting harmony within the Body of Christ, and helping us use our spiritual gifts and resources effectively.

We frown on cliques or exploitation. Instead, we choose to value each other's race, culture, age, gender, and social status without discrimination.

We celebrate our diversity and harmony as a telling demonstration that Jesus' Church Universal—although filled with imperfect people—remains impervious to the gates of Hell.

Social Virtue

God created the human species in His image. We show we're equals by interacting with sincerity, honor, and respect and advancing the cause of the other person's value and dignity. We obey the laws of the land, (except laws that contradict laws of conscience or God's Laws as revealed in Scripture), and we honor and pray for our civic leaders regardless of party affiliation. Our social virtue allows us to extend ourselves to others to form and nurture positive working and learning

> *Working*

As God's faithful stewards in the workplace, we are reliable and responsible. We yield to authority, follow instructions, and do not express petty sentiments toward our coworkers. We are exemplary team players who celebrate achievements. Not gloating or cynical, we are the positive, on time, fastidious workers, who do not defraud the company through malingering. We don't use company resources for personal benefit, we turn in honest reports, and we do not use company time for Bible study or witnessing.[10]

---

[10] Unless it's a part of our job description, we read our Bibles and/or share our faith during scheduled breaks, as permitted and appropriate. Check with your supervisor or HR Department for guidance here.

We may receive recognition for our vocational accomplishments. Some may receive substantial monetary retirement packages, while others may not. God sees us, and as we serve faithfully, we will get His eternal commendation.

> *Learning*

Yearning to grow through formal interactive learning is a worthy endeavor, supported by Scripture. We respect our colleagues, teachers, and administrators. We are punctual, research diligently, and are amenable with peers. We don't cheat on exams or plagiarize. We follow instructions, protect school equipment, and abstain from binge drinking, exhibitionism, sexual promiscuity, or hazing. We complete our assignments and graduate to lifelong endeavors where we make substantive contributions.

God's People Act Differently

Our lives undergo an incredible change in the presence of our holy, almighty God. Moses lived in Egyptian royalty and splendor as Pharaoh's grandson, before he became a murderer, a fugitive, and a vagabond. Yet, this dejected, humiliated sheepherder found the Holy One in the Sinai Desert where his life changed forever.

Removing his shoes to show his submission, Moses began a course of illustrious service. God mandated holiness through this transformed servant. He became an exemplary model to the Children of Israel to be holy because the Lord is holy. Through Moses, we have the ceremonial and judicial principles that influence the religious and social affairs of God's people today.

Seven hundred years later, Isaiah saw God's holiness in the Temple at Jerusalem. There, he had a divine meeting that led to his confession, consecration, and call. Isaiah went to the Temple mourning King Uzziah. He left in awe of God's incomparable attributes,

> Wonderful Counselor, Mighty God, Everlasting Father, and Prince of Peace. (Isaiah 9:6)

Job, David, Peter, Paul, and we show that in God's presence, we instantly distinguish worldly from godly. No longer mundane or common, God becomes our true, holy, almighty Father who gives us loving, fulfilling, and eternal fellowship. Psalm 8 tells us how God made us a little lower than angels, and how He gives us dominion over His creation. God created us with incomparable value to live in harmony with Him,

> If a man love me, he will keep my words: and my Father will love him, and we will come unto him, and make our abode with him. (John 14:23)

We also read in the Scriptures,

> Simon Peter, a servant and an apostle of Jesus Christ, to them that have obtained

like precious faith with us through the righteousness of God and our Savior Jesus Christ: Grace and peace be multiplied unto you through the knowledge of God, and of Jesus our Lord, According as his divine power hath given unto us all things that pertain unto life and godliness, through the knowledge of him that hath called us to glory and virtue: Whereby are given unto us exceeding great and precious promises: that by these ye might be partakers of the divine nature, having escaped the corruption that is in the world through lust. (2 Peter 1:1–4)

Virtue is how we carry out God's will to help others as His loving hands and feet. As we do so, He satisfies our needs as well.

Before looking at knowledge, we'll look at a situation where you are the central character who decides the outcome. After reading, answer the questions and compare them to the answers in the Appendix.

A Problem with Money

Your organization is in financial decline, and you have trouble paying salaries and expenses. An old high school acquaintance calls to invite you to lunch at a local restaurant. You arrive and engage in small talk about your ministry. As she tells you about her software development corporation, you remember hearing about it in recent news reports. They are Fortune 500 executives worth over ten billion dollars.

She tells how your conduct in high school inspired her and her spouse to become Christians. Your noble behavior contrasted with the other students who experimented with drugs and sex. They accepted Christ while attending college and started a software development firm after graduation.

As their business grew, God led them to establish a foundation to support Christian organizations. God led them to donate $1.5 million to your work, with the stipulation that the gift remains anonymous.

Before you leave the restaurant, she embraces you, gives you a leather bag containing the cash, and says, "This is for your ministry. I know you will do the right thing." You thank her, take the leather bag, and return to your car. Several minutes pass as you stare at the bag in dazed disbelief, unable to fathom what has happened.

Scenario Questions: What do you do with the cash? Why?

Knowledge

Chapter Three
Add Knowledge to Your Virtue

The Reverend Dr. L. B. Moss

At the turn of the last century, Leander Bonaparte Moss sought to fight the social issues of his day as an attorney. However, the Lord had other plans for his life. At Houston (later Bishop) College, a young Leander committed himself to a way of Christian service that spanned more than half a century as an accomplished pastor, theologian, and administrator. At the time of his death, the Reverend Dr. L. B. Moss loved three treasures: Jesus Christ, his wife Hattie, and the Park Avenue Missionary Baptist Church, Riverside, California, where he served fifty-seven years as pastor.

Dr. Moss established churches; organized the California State Baptist Convention, Inc., twice serving as president. The California State Baptist District Sunday School and Baptist Training Union Congress, the Providence Baptist Theological Seminary, and the Riverside Seminary were also by-products of his distinguished, fruitful ministry. We admired his aptitude, acuity, and engaging personality. He refrained from using his knowledge to impress or demean. Instead, he produced knowledgeable Christian leaders who practiced 1 Timothy 4:16,

> Take heed unto thyself, and unto the doctrine; continue in them: for in doing this thou shalt both save thyself, and them that hear thee.

Thank you, Papa![11]

What is Knowledge?
Knowledge, or the Greek *gnosis* (Strong-G1108), denotes the information we've accumulated through study. In our age of specialization, we require knowledge and skill to be a qualified professional. Physicians learn medicine, attorneys research law. We Believers examine the Word of God (Bible) to become practitioners of the Christian faith.

Our Lord Jesus possessed and valued knowledge. At twelve, He was in Herod's Temple at Jerusalem, listening to the teachers of the Law and Old Testament traditions and asking questions. (Luke 2:46) Our spiritual existence depends on Christ, the Living Word, who said,

> It is the spirit that quickeneth; the flesh profiteth nothing: the words that I speak unto you, they are spirit, and they are life. (John 6:63)

The Bible helps us to grow spiritually and morally, as David attests,

> Thy word have I hid in mine heart, that I might not sin against thee. (Psalm 119:11)

---

[11] Although we were not blood-related, Dr. Moss called me "Son." Lovingly and respectfully, I called him "Papa."

We cannot read this holy book as we would a newspaper or paperback novel. Instead, we must rely on God to give us the spiritual insight to interpret and apply it properly.

We may pick up nuances from independent study. However, we best learn from spiritually mature Christians who teach the Bible exegetically and "read out" of the Bible God's instruction for us. The antithesis is eisegesis or "reading into" the Bible speculation and subjective opinions that produce Scriptural error, false doctrine, confusion, and controversy. We must pursue sound doctrine and teaching,

> Knowledge does not take twentieth-century people back to first-century ways of living. It brings the universal and timeless truths as redemptive realities for living today. It translates the Jesus of history into the Christ of faith.[12]

Helping Believers draw proper conclusions from the Bible underscores the importance of Christian discipleship.

Our Need for Christian Discipleship

Christian discipleship takes place in the church settings, where we explore the Bible's content, context, and application through Biblical

---

[12] Charles Bryant, *Rediscovering Our Spiritual Gifts* (Nashville: Upper Room Books, 1991), 107.

hermeneutics to avoid biblical speculation and render a true reckoning of God's inspired Word.

In the beginning, *the Enemy* used half-truths and innuendos to dissuade Adam and Eve from pursuing God's words. As in Peter's day, false teachers today deploy the same strategy by adding subtle changes to the Bible through clever phrases and speculation. Instead of drawing conclusions from the Bible's text itself, spurious opinions are for the "itching ears" of 2 Timothy 4:3–4.

We can "rightly divide" (interpret and share) God's Word, as 2 Timothy 2:15 instructs. God will punish us for adding or taking from God's Word as Proverbs 30:5–6 and Revelation 22:18–19 warn us. Much like a carpenter whose screwdriver differs from a claw hammer, we can learn how each book differs in the following diagram:

> *Bible Composition*

The Old Testament (Thirty-Nine Books)	
Five Law Books (Pentateuch/Torah)	Genesis, Exodus, Leviticus, Numbers, & Deuteronomy
Twelve Historical Books	Joshua, Judges, Ruth, 1 & 2 Samuel, 1 & 2 Kings, 1 & 2 Chronicles, Ezra, Nehemiah & Esther
Five Poetical Books	Job, Psalms, Proverbs, Ecclesiastes, & Song of Solomon

Five Major[13] Prophets	Isaiah, Jeremiah, Lamentations, Ezekiel, & Daniel
Twelve Minor Prophets	Hosea, Joel, Amos, Obadiah, Jonah, Micah, Nahum, Habakkuk, Zephaniah, Haggai, Zechariah, & Malachi

The New Testament (Twenty-Seven Books)	
Four Gospels	Matthew, Mark, Luke, & John
One Historical Book	The Acts of the Apostles
Fourteen Letters (Epistles) Attributed to Paul	Romans, 1 & 2 Corinthians, Galatians, Ephesians, Philippians, Colossians, 1 & 2 Thessalonians, 1 & 2 Timothy, Titus, Philemon, & Hebrews
Seven Letters (Epistles) Attributed to Apostles	James, 1 &2 Peter, 1, 2 & 3 John, & Jude
One Apocalyptic Book	The Revelation of Jesus Christ

We can use a Bible version that is easy to read and understand that contains chain references, maps, and concordances. Bible dictionaries, atlases,

---

[13] The terms "Major" and "Minor" denote the length of writings, not the prophet's significance.

commentaries, and other aids are invaluable in our study. Supplemental reference materials (e.g., Old and New Testament surveys, Old and New Testament, Jewish, church, and world histories, systematic theology, Christian doctrine, Hebrew and Greek word studies, dictionaries, etc.) can benefit us as well.

Through Christian discipleship, we learn we are not of this world. God has a plan for us He will complete in His proper time. Six doctrines tell of His incredible purpose in grace.

> *Six Fundamental Christian Doctrines*

God is the one true, living God. He expresses Himself as Father, Son, and Holy Spirit. The Father creates, sustains, and rules Heaven and earth. The Son is Mediator, Redeemer, Savior, and Lord. He secures our atonement by His death and resurrection. The Holy Spirit quickens, comforts, guides, unites us in Christ, guarantees our victory over the Enemy, and secures our place in Heaven.

Jesus Christ is the center of our Christian community. As our Prophet, He inspires us and guides the trajectory of our lives through the biblical accounts of His life and teachings. As our Priest, He forgives, purges, and removes our sins. As our King, He governs our hearts and minds through His Spirit and Word. In Him, we unite, because He is the center of our love, gratitude, and faith.

Our Sin Nature (Sin). God created us in His image to have eternal fellowship. Because of our disobedience, we fell from our innocent state to become sinners. We are without God's righteousness and are amenable to wickedness. Alienated from God and subject to His condemnation, we need a Savior.

The Bible is the Word of God. Inspired individuals penned His sacred words to disclose His divine truths to fallen humanity. It contains principles for human conduct and opinion. It unites the Old Testament, which reveals God's eternal standards through His Law, with the New Testament, which reveals our reconciliation to God through Christ. As we read, study, memorize, and apply its principles, we grow into his productive people of faith and grace.

The Church: As one body in Christ, Christians are the "called out," or in the Greek *ekklesia* (Strong-G1577); a people who are distinct from the world. We unite in prayer, worship, fellowship, Bible study, service, and accountability. We observe its ordinances and rituals that strengthen us. Christian Baptism symbolizes our death to sin and our resurrection to new life. In the Lord's Supper, we use bread and wine to commemorate the Lord's death, and show our dependence on Him for our spiritual life, and looking forward to dining with Him in Heaven as He promised.

In *the World to Come*, our Lord will descend from Heaven to occupy a new Heaven and earth without sin, Satan, or things defiled. A final separation will occur where those of us who trust in Christ will share eternal bliss in Heaven. There we will have His eternal peace, rest, and comfort. Those who have not come to Christ will face eternal torment and separation from God in Hell.

Christian discipleship helps us with vetting candidates for professional ministry. After years of faithful service with a humble and reverent spirit, suitable candidates require honest answers to the question, "What has God called me to do?" Clarifying this question will help free candidates from malevolence or burnout from attempting to "fit" where they are not gifted or prepared.

To ensure God's calling, the candidates spend years under the supervision of an experienced pastor. Then they can glean from the pastor's vast training and experiences to prepare them for navigating the subtle complexities of ministerial service. One's secular acuity does not translate into skillful Christian leadership; the secular worldview must yield to a biblical worldview to achieve lasting, abundant spiritual fruit.

Christian Service
Christian discipleship helps us fulfill Ephesians 4:12, as we equip and edify others. Through unbiased assessments of our strengths and weaknesses, we can identify and use our spiritual gifts effectively in Christian service. There are many spiritual gifts, but we can honor Christ and

benefit our churches and communities using these eight spiritual gifts.

Eight Spiritual Gifts

Helpers (1 Corinthians 12:28) unselfishly share their time, talents, and resources to assist others. Easily recognized, they are first to respond to needs. They also shun recognition, because God will reward them. A fine biblical example is Ruth, who helped Naomi.

Givers (Proverbs 3:27, Romans 12:8, and Galatians 6:10) share their resources unselfishly to meet needs. They, too, respond quickly and prefer anonymity. Givers delight meeting needs without repayment. God provides them resources to share with others. Jesus' parable of the Good Samaritan shows how givers respond to the needs of others.

The Wise (1 Corinthians 12:8 and James 1:5) can see problems from God's perspective, and they respond appropriately. More than human intellect, the wise deliberate and act in ways that glorify God and astound people. Solomon's resolution to the two prostitutes who claimed to be the mother of one infant astonished everyone because it was from God.

Exhorters (Romans 12:8) share Scripture to console discouraged Christians. Without fanfare, exhorters take great pleasure in helping people gain a renewed inspiration and motivation to serve God. Jonathan exhorted David to trust in God and stay on course as the future king of Israel.

Evangelists (Ephesians 4:11) can share Christ with positive results. God calls, equips, and inspires people to serve Him in this capacity. The Bible tells about Philip the evangelist at Caesarea.

Pastors (Jeremiah 3:15, Acts 20:28, Ephesians 4:11, 1 Timothy 3:1–7, and Titus 1:5–16) nurture people toward spiritual maturity. Not recent converts, they are spiritually mature leaders who serve under the authority of Jesus Christ, the Good Shepherd. God serves as both teacher and leader. *As Teacher* (Romans 12:7 and Ephesians 4:11), the pastor explains the Bible so that others can understand and apply to life, just like Jesus, who taught with great effectiveness. *As Leader* (Romans 12:8 and 1 Corinthians 12:28), they give oversight with tact, vision, and prudence to maximize resources and provide direction. God used Moses to shepherd and instruct the Children of Israel while leading them out of Egyptian bondage.[14]

The Importance of Christian Experience

We will have many fulfilling moments that show how God loves, protects and provides for us. We grow confident that He directs our steps and will never leave or forsake us. Our Christian experiences enhance our knowledge and strengthen our faith in God and His Word, and

---

[14] Non-pastors can have the gifts of teaching and leadership and use them in church and/or community service effectively.

not our subjective thoughts or feelings. Our subjectivity has led some to tell how ministers are more effective after they've had a troubled history. Ministry effectiveness is up to God. We can acknowledge our grim history, but as a contrast to the eternal, abundant life that we now have in Christ. (We all need Christian accountability. However, people with years of painful episodes should complete a treatment program before serving. This will lessen the risk of relapse. Counterproductive "baggage" can imperil others to spiritual, physical, emotional, or psychological injury.)

Another misnomer is that numerical church growth, large edifices, and notoriety are *the* indicators of success. Still, this is not a correct assessment. The Lord's plan is mysterious as He raises people as He sees fit. Saving souls, growing in faith, and serving others define ministry effectiveness from His perspective, which is all that matters. The Bible presents how Enoch walked with God daily. (Genesis 5:24) It's possible to accept Christ early and stay with Him for a lifetime. We who follow this pattern are living demonstrations of His miraculous power. Knowledge helps us to sanctify the Lord God in our hearts, so we can give a prompt response to the hope within us with meekness and godly reverence. (1 Peter 3:15)

In this chapter, we explored knowledge. Before exploring temperance, please read the following scenario where you face a moral decision. You may compare your answers to those in the Appendix.

Double Trouble!

After completing your MBA, you become an investment banker to help other Christians with their retirement planning. You become a financial counselor. In just two years, you make junior partner. Your achievement, financial gain, and the positive outcomes from the clients you've helped convince you that you are doing God's will. To prepare for an IRS audit, you review company records and discover that your accounts are 90 percent of the business, of which $125 million is missing. You tell your colleagues and they assure you they will resolve the discrepancy.

FBI agents arrest you for embezzlement, and at your trial, certain documents "prove" you embezzled money to purchase property overseas. The judge sentences you to ten years in federal prison. You arrive at a federal detention facility where you share a cell with an older prisoner who informs you that the firm where you worked laundered money for the mob. On Sunday, your cellmate invites you to chapel services, where the chaplain introduces you as a Christian soldier. He leads you to the front of the room to give your testimony.

Scenario Questions: What should you say/do? Why?

Temperance

Chapter Four
Add Temperance to Your Knowledge

Temperance vs. Self-Indulgence
Asked about the greatest Commandment, Jesus outlines two: to love God with all our heart, soul, and mind, and love our neighbors as we would ourselves. (Matthew 22:36–40, Mark 12:28–34, Luke 10:25–37)

The Lord wants us to live in harmony with God, neighbors, and ourselves, especially when meeting our physical, social, and aesthetic needs. Jesus reinforces a simple rule of life: altruism improves our quality of life; exploitation does not.

Many heretics have postulated godless apostasies that exclude the tenants of Scriptural orthodoxy and fundamental Christianity. Simon Magus offered money to possess the Holy Spirit to enhance his magical power. (Acts 8:13; 18–19) Historians associate the term, "Simony," or purchasing spiritual gifts and graces for personal gain to Simon Magus.

We also attribute to him Christian Gnosticism, which discredits Jesus' redeeming work in favor of "enlightenment" or "special knowledge." Antinomianism or the view that since God saves us with His grace, we are free of all moral obligations is a derivative of "special knowledge" that plagued the church during the First Century A.D.[15]

The church at Corinth was notorious for its licentious conduct, as members engaged in family incest along with sexual liaisons with the Temple of Venus prostitutes, which prompted the chastening in 1 Corinthians 6:9,

> Know ye not that the unrighteous shall not inherit the kingdom of God? Be not deceived: neither fornicators, nor idolaters, nor adulterers, nor effeminate, nor abusers of themselves with mankind, Nor thieves, nor covetous, nor drunkards, nor revilers, nor extortioners, shall inherit the kingdom of God.

Early Christian historians along with modern writers tell about the Nicolaitans, and the overall lascivious climate of the First Century,

> A large proportion of the clergy were notoriously lax on their sex relations and were married or kept concubines. This

---

[15] For further information on Simon Magus and the Christian Gnostic threat, see: Philip Schaff, *Apostolic Christianity A.D. 1-100*, *History of the Christian Church*, reprint, vol. 1, (Grand Rapids: Eerdmans, 1985) 566–568 and Kenneth Scott Latourette, *A History of Christianity: Beginnings to 1500*, rev. ed., vol. 1, (San Francisco: Harper, 1975) 123-125, also see: J.D. Douglas, et al., "Simony," *The Concise Dictionary of the Christian Tradition: Doctrine, Liturgy, History*, (Grand Rapids: Regency, 1989) 349.

was known as nicolaitanism, from a practice denounced in The Revelation of John.[16]

Many yet advocate a brand of religion where the Bible and the Holy Spirit do not govern our conduct and character. It's what feels good that does, as we live conflicted lives, trying to find fulfillment in two opposing worlds. One world has Jesus Christ as its Lord and Savior and offers an abundant, eternal life, while the other world yields to Satan, our impulses, and our egos, producing sin, destruction, and death.

The Bible depicts a time before Christ's return where iniquity abounds, and we have little regard for our fellow human beings. Then we will use people and cherish things while pursuing pride of life, lust of the eyes, and lust of the flesh with great intensity.

Exhibiting tyrannical power/influence without regard best depicts the pride of life. God's design for power and influence is to maintain order, render justice, and help others in need. We resort to violence, brutality, intimidation, maltreatment, domination, and/or suppression to maintain

---

[16] Latourette, 460. See also: Irenaeus, "Against the Heresies," in *The Ante-Nicene Fathers*, vol. 1, ed. Alexander Roberts and James Donaldson, American Edition Reprint, ed. A. Cleveland Coxe, (Grand Rapids: Wm. B. Eerdmans Publishing Company, 1987) 352, and Revelation 2:6.

control. The pride of life can be as subtle as prejudice or as overt as war and can affect all of us directly or indirectly.

The lust of the eyes is amassing valuable items for personal gratification. Love for money is a prime example where we splurge on ourselves, but we are cold and indifferent when others need our generosity or compassion. God's plan is for us to use our financial resources (tithes and offerings) as worship, and to provide for His ministers. God also wants us to be benevolent toward the needy through charitable giving, and to gain financial means for ourselves.

The lust of the flesh is our overindulgence for sensual gratification. Gluttony, substance abuse, and sexual incorrigibility are common forms of this obsession. Sexual incorrigibility contravenes God's plan for the human species to foster and sustain healthy, interpersonal relationships. When we ignore God's biblical model for human sensual fulfillment through the sexual bond, we have false intimacy instead,

> The fantasies of a sex addict are feeble attempts to gain what only God is capable of giving, which we will experience partially on earth and fully in Heaven. Sexual fantasy can conjure up a perfect world of nourishment, love, generosity, and tenderness …The truth is, however, that when we try to bury the core reality of emptiness, the result is false intimacy,

not genuine. When we insist that our needs of intimacy be fulfilled and ignore the reality that loneliness is always present, we get the very opposite of what we're demanding: We're left alone to stare with open eyes at the harsh reality of nakedness.[17]

The Bible presents God's plan for "safe sex," as marital fidelity within a monogamous relationship between a man and woman where the marriage bed is undefiled (Hebrews 13:4) as two individuals become one flesh,

> But from the beginning of the creation God made them male and female. For this cause shall a man leave his father and mother, and cleave to his wife; And they twain shall be one flesh: so then they are no more twain, but one flesh. What therefore God hath joined together, let not man put asunder. (Mark 10:6-9)

Here lies God's wise and intricate design of the nuclear family. He created one male and one female to build trust and commitment through emotional and sexual fidelity; to create and sustain a life-long psychological and physical connection through a spousal love relationship; to foster a

---

[17] Harry W. Schaumburg, *False Intimacy: Understanding the Struggle of Sexual Addiction* (Colorado Springs: NavPress, 1997), 31.

sense of interdependency as the husband and wife "do life together," and propagate humanity through procreation—as God intended in the beginning,

> And the Lord God said, "It is not good that the man should be alone; I will make him an help meet for him." And the Lord God caused a deep sleep to fall upon Adam, and he slept: and he took one of his ribs, and closed up the flesh instead thereof; And the rib, which the Lord God had taken from man, made he a woman, and brought her unto the man. And Adam said, "This is now bone of my bones, and flesh of my flesh: she shall be called Woman, because she was taken out of Man." And they were both naked, the man and his wife, and were not ashamed. (Genesis 2:18–23, 25)

Sexual gratification apart from God's perfect plan yields shattered hopes, destroyed relationships, guilt, shame, and emptiness,

> Don't buy into the promotion of sex as mere physical enjoyment totally apart from the commitment of love. Men who open their Christmas present before the

holiday invariably find themselves bored by the celebration.[18]

Sexual promiscuity is not our identification badge. Jesus gives us His temperance, or the Greek *egkrateia* (Strong-G1466), which is the strength of character to overcome our lusts expressed through inappropriate sexual expression.

My Observation
We admire those who practice a personal self-control by presenting a morally temperate lifestyle to contrast the licentiousness accepted and encouraged by fallen humanity. Christ supplies the tools we need to live sexually responsible,

> For the grace of God that bringeth salvation hath appeared to all men, Teaching us that, denying ungodliness and worldly lusts, we should live soberly, righteously, and godly, in this present world; Looking for that blessed hope, and the glorious appearing of the great God and our Saviour Jesus Christ; Who gave himself for us, that he might redeem us from all iniquity, and purify unto himself a peculiar people, zealous of good works. (Titus 2:11–14)

---

[18] Ted W. Engstrom and Norman B. Rohrer, *Making the Right Choices: Maintaining Your Integrity in a World of Compromise* (Nashville: Thomas Nelson Publishers, 1993), 32.

Through Christ, we now share a willingness to honor Him, serve others, and satisfy our desires safely and appropriately. He transformed us from the inside out and released us from sin's bondage so that we can walk in His Spirit. (Romans 8:1)

Occasionally, temptation may lead to sin. However, the Holy Spirit empowers us take ownership of our transgression(s), reconcile with the offended, and strengthen our resolve to walk with Him even closer (as outlined in Chapters One and Two).

Over time, we develop a growing moral consciousness with fruit that validates our Christian witness,

> There must be a sincere change in one's lifestyle. A person who has genuinely repented will stop doing evil and begin to live righteously. Along with a change of mind and attitude, true repentance will begin to produce a change in conduct. [19]

Joseph, in the Old Testament, had temperance with Potiphar's wife, observing how sex with her was an offense against Potiphar and God. In Christ, we can show chastity with His omnipotent Spirit empowering us.

---

[19] John F. McArthur, *The Gospel According to Jesus*, rev. ed. (Grand Rapids: Zondervan Publishing House, 1994), 182.

In college, there were students who did the "sex-party" life. I thank God my Christian classmates who shared my view that women are God's gift to humanity and that relationships are possible without the pressure of sex. As God's gift to men, we are to respect and appreciate women. Casual dating is one way we can form lasting friendships with women—not opportunities to "score."

Many of us chose not to "party" because it was inconsistent with our commitment to Christ and detrimental to our Christian witness. Further, as a minister, it is hypocritical to preach to my Christian sisters about living for the Christ and obeying His Word, and yet treat them like whores. Over time, my association with those Christian classmates who advocated platonic dating philosophies helped me to develop and preserve a reputation as a gentleman, and it led me to the woman I eventually married.

A classmate invited me to his church, and when I went, the Lord changed my life. I was sitting about the middle of the sanctuary when the service began. I did not attend church that day looking for a wife, but the choir director captivated my attention. For me, it was love at first sight, and the moment I saw her, I heard God speaking to me, "She's the one."

Proverbs 18:22 reads, "Whoso findeth a wife findeth a good thing, and obtaineth favour of the Lord," and those words have been true. From that time until now, through the good and not-so-good times, I am grateful for His special gift in my wife, helper, best friend, companion, and lover—for life. God's temperance gives hope to people struggling with sexual promiscuity as we establish appropriate sexual boundaries,

> What matters in the forbidden zone is not keeping sexual thoughts away, but maintaining a boundary against sexual contact so that the unique potential of these relationships can be realized.[20]

We point people to Christ so they can have His help and healing and not drag sexual "baggage" into their personal and/or professional relations with others.

Jesus teaches how it's possible to abstain from sex while Paul viewed celibacy as our chance to dedicate our lives to the Lord. People can have total fulfillment being "married" to the Lord Jesus Christ. (Matthew 19:12, 1 Corinthians 7:32-35)

Indiscriminate sexual conduct has led to public scandal and disgrace for many well-meaning people of faith. Hedonism (the pursuit of pleasure) does not give lasting fulfillment. It is far better to yield to Christ for a lifetime, because His reward will always yield greater satisfaction.

---

[20] Peter Rutter, MD, *Sex in the Forbidden Zone* (New York: Fawcett Crest Books, 1989), 64.

Before we explore patience, please read the following scenario. You are the person who makes a moral decision. Once you answer the questions, compare yours to the ones in the Appendix.

What's It Worth?
The CEO has been grooming you for his position for ten years. He calls you to his office where he offers you his position. He wants you to attend the company's annual three-day conference across country, where he will make your promotion official. He tells you about his "therapeutic" affair that helps him overcome the sexual inhibitions he's been having with his wife.

He's arranged for you to meet his mistress' friend, who's expressed a desire to connect with you sexually. He gives you a travel voucher with a first-class airline tickets, a company car, hotel reservations, and $5,000 in spending cash. He leans back in his chair and waits for your response.

Scenario Questions: What do you say and do? Why?

Patience

Chapter Five
Add Patience to Your Temperance

Who Shall Endure?

Christians have debated two views on the eternal security. One group insists none of us can be certain of obtaining eternal life. We will not persevere and will renounce our faith. The opposing group shares Peter's view that we will endure patiently; the Greek *hupomone* (Strong-G5281), or persevere, and our eternal life is absolute.

The difference between the groups is where we place our faith and confidence. For the former group, we place our hope and confidence in our capricious human will and our finite strength. Here, it is up to us to hold on to Christ the best way *we* can as we face life's uncertainties.

In the latter view, our faith and confidence is on God's infinite power and providence, and it's up to Him to hold on to us the best way *He* can as we live our lives, dependent on Him as the New Hampshire Confession reads,

> We believe the Scriptures teach that such as are truly regenerate, being born of the Spirit, will not utterly fall away and perish, but will endure to the end; that their persevering attachment to Christ is the grand mark which distinguishes them from superficial professors; that a special Providence watches over their welfare;

and that they are kept by the power of God through faith unto salvation. [21]

The Good Shepherd knows His sheep; they follow Him, and He gives them eternal life. They will never perish, and no one can take them out of His almighty hands. (John 10:27-28) We endure patiently because we focus on Christ, whose providence watches over us while His preservation keeps us.

God's Providence and Preservation

God is Creator and Sovereign Ruler of Heaven and earth. His Providence is the continual expression of His omnipresence, omnipotence, and omniscience as He carries out His divine plan for the universe and everything in it. From creation to the culmination of all things, no human activity or event in nature escapes His supervision and care,

> God's vital power so pervades the universe that "in him we live, and move, and have our being." Acts xvii. 28. I know not how language can express more forcibly the idea of dependence on God than do the words of Paul in his discourse to the Athenians. He teaches that this dependence is so absolute that apart from

---

[21] See Hiscox, 67 and J. Newton Brown, *A Baptist Church Manual*, 37th ed. (Valley Forge: Judson, 1983), 15.

God there is in us no life, no motion, no existence. Separation from him would extinguish the mysterious principle called life, would arrest all motion, and put an end to existence. [22]

Scripture tells how God's providential care extends to His precious children,

> Because thou hast made the LORD, which is my refuge, even the most High, thy habitation; There shall no evil befall thee, neither shall any plague come nigh thy dwelling. For he shall give his angels charge over thee, to keep thee in all thy ways. They shall bear thee up in their hands, lest thou dash thy foot against a stone. (Psalm 91:9-12)

The Scriptures also declare,

> And we know that all things work together for good to them that love God, to them who are the called according to his purpose. (Romans 8:28)

God's preservation complements His providence as He sustains us forever,

---

[22] James Madison Pendleton, *Christian Doctrines, A Compendium of Theology*, 33rd printing, (Philadelphia: Judson Press, 1976) 129.

> Thou, even thou, art LORD alone; thou hast made heaven, the heaven of heavens, with all their host, the earth, and all things that are therein, the seas, and all that is therein, and thou preservest them all; and the host of heaven worshippeth thee. (Nehamiah 9:6)

Nothing escapes God's watchfulness, foreknowledge, and preservation of our conception and birth, occurrences in life, and the time of our death, and He even numbers each of our hair follicles. (Matthew 10:30) Having such a caring, precise, compassionate Heavenly Father controlling our lives—not fate, chance, karma, luck, or happenstance—should evoke our greatest assurance and confidence, as we understand that one day, He shall reveal His divine purpose and answer every question of the human heart,

> For we know in part, and we prophesy in part. But when that which is perfect is come, then that which is in part shall be done away. (1 Corinthians 13: 9-10)

Further,

> And I heard a great voice out of heaven saying, Behold, the tabernacle of God is with men, and he will dwell with them, and they shall be his people, and God himself shall be with them, and be their God. And God shall wipe away all tears from their eyes; and there shall be no more death, neither sorrow, nor crying, neither shall there be any more pain: for

the former things are passed away. (Revelation 21:3-4)

His ways are mysterious as He oversees and provides for His creation, even through natural disasters, and our corrupted human autonomy witnessed in barbarism, tyranny, and genocide. Yet His viewpoint is eternal and omniscient, and His ways are transcendent and flawless. He will move in our best interest with goodness and mercy in every situation we face.

God will not give us everything we want. However, He will supply our needs to carry out His perfect will. We can know He hears us, and as we seek Him, we receive His peace and satisfaction. (Matthew 6:33)

We can trust Him daily, surrendering our cares, concerns to His matchless power so that He shows Himself faithful to solve every problem and meet every need. God is in control and not us. We can commit our ways to Him; trust Him, and He will bring it to pass, according to His will. (Psalm 37:5) The Lord promises to keep us, and the Creator and Sustainer of the universe will keep His word as we seek Him.

A Persevering Attachment to Christ
A verbal profession alone does not verify our fellowship with Christ. God will save those who confess Him with their mouths and believe Him with their hearts. (Romans 10:9-10) Profession without belief is worthless. It does not yield a

spiritual transformation or fellowship with God. When the Lord returns, He will banish them from His presence. They're not of Christ and will not endure,

> They went out from us, but they were not of us; for if they had been of us, they would no doubt have continued with us: but they went out, that they might be made manifest that they were not all of us. (1 John 2:19)

We who profess and believe in Him, He preserves forever. He is our hope, strength, and victory as progress along life's journey towards our glorious Heavenly home.

After feeding the multitudes, a crowd sought Jesus for more food. He explained He was the *Bread of Life* and those who follow Him would never hunger or thirst. Then He announced He could meet our earthly needs and those beyond the grave,

> And this is the will of him that sent me, that every one which seeth the Son, and believeth on him, may have everlasting life: and I will raise him up at the last day. (John 6:40)

The crowd walked away from Jesus; insisting that what He proposed was something far too difficult for any person to understand. As they left Him, they took many of His professed followers with them. Therefore, the Lord looked at His Twelve Disciples and asked if they were going to leave

Him as well. Speaking for the Disciples, and for all Christians everywhere, Peter replies,

> Lord, to whom shall we go? Thou hast the words of eternal life. And we believe and are sure that thou art that Christ, the Son of the living God. (John 6:68–69)

No one loves us so deeply, gives Himself so freely and keeps us completely, as does Christ. We pursue Christ because He presents us to God as our,

> Advocate, Alpha and Omega, Bridegroom, Deliverer, Faithful and True Witness, Lord and God, Good Shepherd, Great God and Savior, Great High Priest, Hope of Glory, I Am, Eternal Judge, Friend, King of Glory, Lamb of God, Light of the World, Physician, Prince of Peace, Prophet, Ransom, Redeemer, Resurrection and Life, Righteous Judge, Rock, Ruler of Kings, Savior, True Vine, Truth, Way, and Word of God.

Jesus Christ is our Eternal Keeper, and our patient endurance is more about His faithfulness than about our feeble attempts to hold on to Him,

> Christ's omnipresence makes it possible for Him to be united to, and to be present in each believer, as perfectly and fully as if that believer were the only one to receive Christ's fullness ... each believer has the whole Christ with him as his source of

strength, purity, life; so that each may say: Christ gives all his time and wisdom and care to me. Such a union as this lacks every element of instability. Once formed, the union is indissoluble. Many of the ties of earth are rudely broken—not so with our union with Christ—that endures forever. Since there is now an unchangeable and divine element in us, our salvation depends no longer upon our unstable wills, but upon Christ's purpose and power. [23]

Because Christ persevered and triumphed, we have victory with the promise that no weapon formed against us will prosper. (Isaiah, 54:17) We aren't invincible, for even the Lord's Apostles faced persecution and martyrdom. The Holy Spirit abides within to comfort us in our persecution and suffering. (John 14:16-18)

The Apostle John lived with the Lord three years along with his fellow Apostles, now gone. He witnessed Pentecost and the New Testament church. Despite his exile and tyrannical Roman persecution, John persevered, as Jesus prayed,

> Holy Father, keep through thine own name those whom thou hast given me, that they may be one, as we are. While I was with them in the world, I kept them

---

[23] Strong, 801.

> in thy name: those that thou gavest me I have kept, and none of them is lost, but the son of perdition; that the scripture might be fulfilled. (John 17:11b–12)

We may doubt the Lord's goodness. But He has not abandoned us. Our hardships do not negate God's love, grace, and mercy, nor do they "prove" His desertion. Our toils and disappointments remind us we live in a sinful world, which contrasts our glorious, eternal home. Thus, we can count it all joy because He preserves us for an unspeakable treasure in Heaven. There, all our earthly pain, toil, and suffering will vanish instantly; completely obliterated by the light of Jesus Christ in His full majestic splendor and glory, as Revelation 21:1-5 depicts.

We can be steadfast and vigilant as we pursue our incorruptible inheritance. God keeps us by His power through faith unto salvation, ready to be revealed in the last time. (1 Peter 1:3–5)

In this chapter, we explored our patient endurance. Before exploring godliness, let's take a fictional look at a missionary, a preacher, and an old man.

A Missionary, a Preacher, and an Old Man
While walking through town, Jesus invited people to Heaven, but no one responded. He thought, "I'll go to the missionary, she will be eager to go to Heaven!" It was early afternoon when the Lord arrived at the missionary's beachfront

condominium. He rang the doorbell, but no answer; another ring and still no answer.

As the Lord turned to walk away, he heard the door open and a woman's voice ask, "Who are you? And what do you want?" The Lord turned to see the missionary peering through a partially opened door wearing a nightgown.

Hanging on the closet door behind her was the white missionary uniform she wore for meetings and crusades around the world. On the living room table was the Bible she often carried, with her favorite passage highlighted,

> For by grace are ye saved through faith; and that not of yourselves: it is the gift of God: Not of works, lest any man should boast. For we are his workmanship, created in Christ Jesus unto good works, which God hath before ordained that we should walk in them. (Ephesians 2:8–10)

The Lord said, "I'm the Lord Jesus, and I've come to take you to Heaven!" Slowly, the missionary dropped her head, turned, and closed the door.

Saddened but undaunted, the Lord visited the preacher, who lived across town. It was around late afternoon when He arrived at the preacher's mansion, and knocked on the door. No answer; He knocked a second and third time, and still no answer.

Then as He turned, He heard the door open and the preacher yell, "Who are you? And what do you want?" The Lord could smell the alcohol on the preacher's breath as he stood there with red eyes and slurred speech—growing ever-more impatient with his unwanted, uninvited guest. On the table behind him, the Lord could see the preacher's sermon notes for a message entitled, "The Dangers of Drinking." His Bible was open to this passage,

> Who hath woe? who hath sorrow? who hath contentions? who hath babbling? who hath wounds without cause? who hath redness of eyes? They that tarry long at the wine; they that go to seek mixed wine. (Proverbs 23:29–30)

The Lord said, "I'm the Lord Jesus, and I've come to take you to Heaven!" The preacher threatened, "Get off my property before I call the cops!" and slammed the door.

Saddened, but undaunted, the Lord would visit the old man, who lived in a small home at the end of a deserted road. He's been living there alone since his wife died ten years ago. The kids have moved away, and most of his friends were dead or had moved away as well. Yet the old man was not alone. He found companionship in listening to the Christian radio stations and family programs that evoked many precious memories of a bygone era. Yet, his closest companion was his old, tattered Bible he read every evening. He found inspiration, hope, and joy as he read,

> Let not your heart be troubled: ye believe in God, believe also in me. In my Father's house are many mansions: if it were not so, I would have told you. I go to prepare a place for you. And if I go and prepare a place for you, I will come again, and receive you unto myself; that where I am, there ye may be also. (John 14:1-3)

The old man could read his Bible on this evening. For some inexplicable reason, he had to go outside and stand on the front porch. It was late in the day, and the sun was setting. Nevertheless, the old man could see the shadowy silhouette of a man walking toward the house. As the shadowy figure drew closer to the front gate, he recognized his honored guest. *It was the Lord!*

With great excitement and tears of joy, the old man hurried across the yard into the arms of Jesus and said, "Lord! I love you, and I am so glad to see you. Let's go to Heaven!" Embracing the Old Man, the Lord replied tenderly,

> Well done, thou good and faithful servant: thou hast been faithful over a few things, and I will make thee ruler over many things: enter thou into the joy of thy Lord. (Matthew 25:21)

The old man walked with his Lord down the road, joyfully chatting together. They are still walking and talking today—not on earth, but in Heaven!

Godliness

Chapter Six
Add Godliness to Your Patience

God's Holiness and Our Godliness

Many people use the euphemism "the man upstairs" to describe God; we cannot describe Him as we would a human being. Our remarkable God has many distinctive characteristics that set Him apart from anything we know or can imagine.

Whenever we use His personal name, YHWH, in our King James Bible, we make it the uppercase LORD. [24] God used its derivative, "I Am that I Am," when He charged Moses with leading the Children of Israel. So sacred is His name that when the Lord Jesus Christ applied it to Himself, He infuriated the crowd who heard Him. (John 8:58–59, Exodus 3:14) Our God has many distinctive characteristics that help us appreciate His incomparable majesty and splendor.

Eternal: Our God is eternal, without beginning or end. He always was and will forever be the everlasting God.

---

[24] For further discussion on God's sacred name (or Tetragrammaton), see R. Laird Harris, Gleason L. Archer, and Bruce K. Waltke, *Theological Workbook of the Old Testament*, vol. 1, 2nd ed. (Chicago: Moody Press, 1981), 210–212, and W. E. Vine, Merrill F. Unger, and William White, *Vine's Expository Dictionary of Biblical Words* (Nashville: Thomas Nelson, Inc., 1985), 140–141.

Self-existent: God exists in and of Himself. He alone is the origin of all life as the living God.

Omnipotent and Omniscient: Our God has all power and all knowledge. He can do anything with unlimited, perfect, and eternal knowledge of everything past, present, and future to get His perfect outcome.

Omnipresent: God is everywhere without diminishing His being or essence. He occupies both Heaven and earth fully and simultaneously.

Faithful and True: God is reliable and authentic as the embodiment of truth and veracity, and the source of all that is authentic and genuine.

Just and Righteous: Our God is the source of all moral uprightness, and His right judgments evoke our confidence in every situation.

Loving, Good, and Merciful: Our God loves us with an unfailing and unselfish love. He is good and merciful to forgive sin and restore our eternal fellowship with Him, through Jesus Christ.

Holy: Our God is morally and spiritually perfect. Holiness is the very core of His being. The Hebrew word *qadosh* (Strong-H6918), used in the Old Testament, presents God as the pure, undefiled quality of essence that is completely separated ("cut off") from any other. The Greek counterpart *hagios* (Strong-G40), used in the New Testament, presents God as pure and sacred. Whether studying the Old or New Testament, God is pure, majestic, glorious, and holy without equal.

At Sinai, Moses asked God to show Himself. God warned him that human beings could not behold His glory and put Moses in a cleft on the mount. Then God allowed Moses to see His back as He passed. Moses' brief glimpse of God's backside illuminated his face so much that he had to cover his face from the people to keep from frightening them. (Exodus 34:28–35, 2 Corinthians 3:12–18) After Pentecost, Peter and John healed the lame man at the Jerusalem Temple. The miracle baffled the Jewish leaders as "they marveled; and they took knowledge of them, that they had been with Jesus." (Acts 4:13) When we have a reverent devotion for God (and *get real with Him*), His captivating radiance becomes visible through us.

We also develop a craving for deeper intimacy with God as well. Each day, it becomes easier to invite Him to reign in every area of our lives so that He can show His holiness through us. God commands us to be holy, as He is holy. God is a life-changing Spirit whose majesty and splendor compels us to revere Him. This is our godliness, or the Greek *eusebeia* (Strong-G2150).

Like virtue (Chapter Two), godliness involves a specific and intentional resolve. However, while virtue is what we do, godliness is who (and whose) we are.

Human effort does not produce godliness. Nor does wealth and prestige influence it any more than a "generational curse" causes one's poverty or hardships. Godliness reveals the Holy Spirit's work in us. Much like a compass needle signifies northern magnetic forces, our godliness points to God, who is working in us.

Godliness Revealed
Our godliness is intentional, and we devote ourselves to things that help us grow closer to the Lord. This means putting forth the effort to please God through faith and spiritual due diligence. Using our spiritual gifts under the guidance of pastors and spiritual leaders in a church setting (presented in Chapter Three), we learn how we further God's Kingdom as outlined in the *Beatitudes* of Jesus' *Sermon on the Mount.* (Matthew 5:3–12)

➢ Godliness in the Beatitudes

With humility (*poor in spirit*), we receive the Kingdom of Heaven, as our repentance (*mourn*) helps us receive God's eternal consolation and forgiveness.

Our strength under control (*meek*) helps us secure all that this world offers as God satisfies our yearnings for Him (*hunger and thirst after righteousness*).

We can express pity (*merciful*) because God has done so with us. A wholesome demeanor (*pure in heart*) coupled with our goodwill (*peacemakers*) affirms our identity as God's children who will be with Him soon.

Our allegiance to Christ may cause some people to misunderstand, criticize, and mistreat us (*reviled and persecuted*). Yet, we can rejoice in the Lord always, because we will have His eternal bliss.

Godliness in the Fruit of the Spirit
The *Fruit of the Spirit* (Galatians 5:22–23) is also how God uses us to express godliness. Here, *love* enables us to share unselfish benevolence with those around us (see Chapter Eight).

Our *joy* is the delight that we experience through our fulfilling union with the Good Shepherd, in whom we lack nothing in this life or in the next.

We can seek to create and preserve *peace* because the Prince of Peace helps us endure to the end, which is our *long-suffering* (Chapter Five).

We show *gentleness* in civility. Not insisting on always having our way, we seek the best interest of others as well.

Goodness is intervening for good, as Christ does for us. *Faith* extends beyond believing (Chapter One) to include faithfulness in our commitments.

Meekness reflects a humble submission to God's will, as did our Lord. *Temperance* (Chapter Four) is how we exhibit self-control when our lusts crave gratification.

› Godliness as Prophet, Priest, and King

Ours can be an inspirational witness to Jesus' life and character as expressions of His prophetic, priestly, and kingly roles.

We further Christ's prophetic role through a Bible-based perspective. We can get advice from secular experts, but the Word of God remains the lamp for our feet, which lights our pathways daily. (Psalm 119:105)

We show His priestly role as we consecrate ourselves to God through obedient, sacrificial living where the Lord is center. Jesus says we have to deny ourselves, take up our cross, and follow Him. (Mark 8:34)

We show His kingly role through responsible and accountable living. We interact with others with dignity and respect, using the Bible as our guide. Violence and exploitation can't exist where Christ reigns and His people live out a pure religion that is undefiled, as we provide care and remain unspotted by the world. (James 1:27)

Godliness embodies our Lord's work and will for us, because we know that the unrighteous shall not inherit the Kingdom of God. The Lord purchased us, and we belong to Him. Ultimately, godliness helps us express our love for the Lord, and we seek to please him, because it is the right thing to do.

Before exploring the importance of brotherly kindness, please read the following scenario where you make a moral decision. You may compare your scenario answers to the ones featured in the Appendix.

For the Sake of the Call

For twenty-two years, you have developed and taught within the Christian education ministry at your church. You've taught with modest success, and you feel underappreciated; you feel God wants your ministry to expand.

During your evening Bible study, Influential Member, who's been attending your study, asks to meet after class, and you consent. Influential compliments you for explaining the Bible and complex theological issues. Then, Influential tells you that God brought you both together to "take your ministry to the next level." Influential will leverage resources to publish and distribute your books, videos, and DVDs. Influential has ties to every major Christian conference worldwide with radio, TV, and internet exposure.

Influential gives you an envelope with keys to your luxury car and estate in an exclusive area in town. However, to secure the deal, you must leave your spouse and kids and move into the mansion before the end of the month.

Scenario Questions: What do you say and do? Why?

Brotherly Kindness

Chapter Seven
Add Brotherly Kindness to Your Godliness

From Partiality to Family

Whenever we Christians replace Christ-centered ideals with world-centered ones, we lose our exceptional Christian witness. One example is prejudice, which gives people an excuse for not living in harmony. (This product of the depraved heart is not the product of the new heart that God gives us the moment we come to Christ.)

The Bible depicts Christians as a united group, serving the one true God,

> Endeavouring to keep the unity of the Spirit in the bond of peace. There is one body, and one Spirit, even as ye are called in one hope of your calling; One Lord, one faith, one baptism, One God and Father of all, who is above all, and through all, and in you all. (Ephesians 4:3–6)

Unfortunately, too many of us resist having fellowship with other Christians who are not of the same race, culture, or class, although we share the same Lord and Savior—Jesus Christ. How can we say we are one body and be so fragmented? Brothers and sisters, this should not be!

Then again, prejudice is not a recent phenomenon in the New Testament church. 1 Corinthians 1:10–13 scolds the church for its factions,

> Now I beseech you, brethren, by the name of our Lord Jesus Christ, that ye all speak the same thing and that there be no divisions among you; but that ye be perfectly joined together in the same mind and in the same judgment. For it hath been declared unto me of you, my brethren, by them which are of the house of Chloe, that there are contentions among you. Now this I say, that every one of you saith, I am of Paul; and I of Apollos; and I of Cephas [Peter]; and I of Christ. Is Christ divided? was Paul crucified for you? or were ye baptized in the name of Paul?

Peter faced a similar problem. Fifty days after the Lord's Resurrection, on the Day of Pentecost, the Holy Spirit filled Jesus' followers assembled in Jerusalem. As the New Testament church grew, Jewish traditionalists (Judaizers), sought to preserve Jewish tradition within Christianity.

Gentiles (non-Jews) had to keep God's Law and Jewish traditions as well. They were God's chosen who safeguarded the Law—and Christianity, since Jesus Christ was a Jew. Thus, circumcision and other rituals were mandatory for all Christians.

Then at Joppa, God showed Peter there's no partiality in Christ when Cornelius, a gentile, and his family experienced the Holy Spirit similar to what happened in Jerusalem on Pentecost.

God calls all Christians into His family, where we can practice a fervent, brotherly kindness, or the Greek *philadelphia* (Strong-G5360), toward each other. This horizontal dimension of our vertical faith in Christ enables us to fulfill His prayer for our unity as a caring Christian family,

> And the glory which thou gavest me I have given them; that they may be one, even as we are one: I in them, and thou in me, that they may be made perfect in one; and that the world may know that thou hast sent me, and hast loved them, as thou hast loved me. (John 17:22–23)

We cannot repair 2,000 years of factions and infighting. Yet, we can act as one body in Christ by focusing on what unites us, instead of what divides us. Let us be one Christian family united in love.

We Are a Christian Family
Christians can express genuine affection toward other Christians as we share our joys and offer encouragement, support, and aid to each other when distressed, because the Holy Spirit compels us to do so. As a Christian family, we can change the world around us when we show the following characteristics.

> *The Christian Family Fellowships Together*

We are a diverse people with Christ at the center, called to practice a loving fellowship, or Greek *koinonia* (Strong-G2842). This miracle of simultaneous unity and diversity validates our distinctive message of God's grace and love. Christians yearn for opportunities to connect because we enjoy our Christian family. The world is a cold, cruel, and lonely place, where smiles are rare, and where people are so busy that they do not have time to establish and maintain connections. We share Sunday dinners, celebrate birthdays and special occasions, and attend events of mutual interest. In this way, we can show the world that we are a family where no one is a stranger or outcast.

> *The Christian Family Helps Each Other*

We Christians share the responsibility to honor and prefer one another as Romans 12:10 teaches. Through food and benevolent programs, we care for each other tangibly and meaningfully. We also follow the Lord, who said, "Inasmuch as ye have done it unto one of the least of these my brethren, ye have done it unto me." (Matthew 25:40b)

Both the donor and recipient have a tremendous obligation within the Christian family. The donor must assist the recipient in need, as much as possible, as an extension of God's loving hands. The recipient must have a legitimate need and is not deceiving the donor. It would be unconscionable for a person to request financial help when the "real" motive is to support high-risk behavior.

It is never a healthy exchange to lie about needing money to pay for food, rent/mortgage, car note, utilities, etc., when it's for a drug/alcohol habit, gambling debt, or the person feels entitled and is above having to work to support themselves.[25] The recipient must never exploit the donor, as God will punish those who exploit His precious children.

I recall when it was difficult to finance seminary. Years had passed since my college graduation, and I was working and raising a family. Then the Lord connected me with someone who paid my graduate tuition. That experience taught me five valuable lessons. I learned God makes impossible dreams possible. I learned to extend help to others in need. I learned financial accountability through submitting regular progress reports. I learned humility by watching the donor refuse all public recognition of his generosity. Moreover, I learned that Christian brotherly kindness transcends race and culture because Jesus Christ is at the center.

The Christian Family Supports Each Other

Ours is a caring community of faith. We pray for and give support as a listening ear, a shoulder to

---

[25] Here, giving is poor stewardship. It would be better to refer the recipient to a church ministry, Christian nonprofit, counseling service, or social service agency that can address the issue or issues.

cry on, a pat on the back, or wise counsel when needed. We do not stockpile ammunition for gossip against our weakened brothers and sisters. Unless it's a reportable issue, we keep others' confidences safe, or we ask for permission to share with professionals who can intervene appropriately.

Two Christian brothers, "Michael" and "Gabriel," were instrumental in my becoming a minister. I was active in church and in community service when a pastor recommended a college to me, and I enrolled a few months later. During my first year, I met Michael, a minister from another country, and we became friends. As time passed, he would challenge me, "*You ought to be a preacher!*" I thought little of his challenges until one November evening when his words pricked my heart, when I heard the Lord speak through him, calling me to ministerial service. Later that evening, I became a minister, and the next time I saw Michael, I explained what happened and thanked him for his advice. He was very pleased.

Several months before I became a minister, another minister and I attended a worship service where the pastor encouraged congregants to assemble at the altar for prayer, and I went forward. Many people came forward uttering ecstatically, as many faith traditions have as their custom today. Then, during the prayer, the person standing in front of me turned and said God wanted me saved. I experienced salvation years before, so I said nothing and continued praying. I exited the building shortly after the prayer.

While standing in the parking lot with my minister friend, we met Gabriel. What happened next is still a blur. Yet, what I remember went something like this. After exchanging pleasantries, Gabriel looked up to the sky and uttered the most beautiful language I've ever heard. (I could discern it was a language, but I'm not sure if anyone on earth speaks that dialect.) Once he finished the utterance, he looked at us and said in English something about us being ministers, and that we would serve the Lord for the rest of our lives. We then parted company, and I never saw Gabriel again.

Many years have passed since my encounter with Gabriel. The Bible teaches we should be cordial to strangers since we may entertain angels unawares. (Hebrews: 13:2) Whether Gabriel was an angel, I cannot tell. I can say that I have not forgotten that meeting, or the one with Michael.

The Christian Family Shows Genuine Affection for Each Other

Jesus Christ is a friend who sticks closer than a brother does, and He equips us to care for each other. Expressing our affection is easy because we see each other through the eyes of Jesus Christ, who laid down His life for His friends. Whenever we meet other Christians, the Holy Spirit in us makes us feel comfortable almost instantly, even though we've never met. We share the same Lord, who makes us one, just as He is one with His Father. With brotherly kindness, we contrast the snobbery and prejudice this fallen world accepts and advocates.

As we fellowship—in peaceful coexistence—we dispel the false notion that diversity will only produce hatred, ill will and discord within the Christian family. We have a distinct Christian witness that verifies our fellowship with God.

We display how God loves and seeks reconciliation with a sin-cursed human race as we treat each other with the utmost respect, acceptance, and honor. Our affection is not optional—it is compulsory, because the world craves this unifying message of acceptance of others through Christ. We offer a glimpse of Heaven, a rich diversity of people, as John saw on the Isle of Patmos,

> After this I beheld, and, lo, a great multitude, which no man could number, of all nations, and kindreds, and people, and tongues, stood before the throne, and before the Lamb, clothed with white robes, and palms in their hands; And cried with a loud voice, saying, Salvation to our God which sitteth upon the throne, and unto the Lamb. (Revelation 7:9–10)

Jesus is returning, because we are precious in His sight. Can't we value each other equally and see each other through His gracious and forgiving eyes? *I believe we can!* We may disagree about dogma or our form of worship, but we can look beyond our human-made differences to unite in Christ to show we are blood-washed and blood-bought saints. Just as the Lamb's eternal glory will unite us in Heaven, our brotherly kindness can unite us on earth.

Before looking at love, please read the following scenario and imagine you have to make a moral decision. You can compare your answers to those presented in the Appendix.

A True Friend
After high school, you become a summer missionary where a couple befriends you as you perform short-term ministry. After summer, you decide to stay in the area and soon become the Missions Director at the church. You do an exceptional job as director for eight years, when the host couple makes unsubstantiated character assassinations against you to the church about your "hidden sin." They insist you either resign or suffer the consequences. You deny any wrongdoing, but the church dismisses you at their recommendation.

Years later, while serving as lead pastor at another church, the same couple joins the church. They are without money, housing, or employment, and you secure their housing and pay their lease for the first six-months. You secure employment with competitive salary and benefits, provide food, clothing, show them schools, recreation, and hospitals in the area, and do all you can to get them settled.

After church, they invite you to dinner, where they ask for your forgiveness and prayer. You pray for them and reassure them you forgave them long ago. Fifteen years have passed, and you are the best of friends.

Scenario Questions: Was this the right response? What would you have done? Why?

Love

Chapter Eight
Add Love to Your Brotherly Kindness

A New Commandment

Love has many meanings. It can name an emotional attraction for job, house, vehicles, classical music, pizza, that odd Christmas sweater, and that pair of comfortable jeans. To the Greeks, we can express parental (*storge*), fraternal (*phileo*), or sensual (*eros*) love. However, Jesus transcends these concepts when He establishes this new paradigm,

> A new commandment I give unto you, That ye love one another; as I have loved you, that ye also love one another. By this shall all men know that ye are my disciples, if ye have love one to another. (John 13:34-35)

The Greek *agape* (Strong-G26), is the highest form of pure love because God is its power source. Our Lord is holy, and His love is without sin and selfishness. We are incapable of such pure altruistic love with our human strength alone, since our love seeks reciprocation. The Holy Spirit's power makes it possible—although difficult—for Christians to express God's agape love in ways that serve the recipient's best interests. Similar to the brotherly kindness (Chapter Seven), which we share with other Christians, we can extend agape love even to our enemies, as Jesus says,

Ye have heard that it hath been said, Thou shalt love thy neighbor, and hate thine enemy. But I say unto you, Love your enemies, bless them that curse you, do good to them that hate you, and pray for them which despitefully use you, and persecute you; That ye may be the children of your Father which is in heaven: for he maketh his sun to rise on the evil and on the good, and sendeth rain on the just and on the unjust. For if ye love them which love you, what reward have ye? do not even the publicans the same? And if ye salute your brethren only, what do ye more than others? do not even the publicans so? Be ye therefore perfect, even as your Father which is in heaven is perfect. (Matthew 5:43–48)

God's Love Becomes Human

The Bible tells us that God is love (1 John 4:8), and He continues to express it unselfishly. In the beginning, He created a perfect habitation for imperfect humans. After we fell and sin contaminated the world, He showed mercy to Adam and Eve through a promised Redeemer, who would nullify sin's curse and dominion forever.

God's love preserved humanity through Noah, when sin was rampant in the earth. Later, He produced a people of faith through Abraham to be a blessing to others. God's love motivated Him to deliver His people from Egyptian bondage, part the Red Sea, give them His Law, feed them in the wilderness for 40 years, and give them a "Promised Land." His love foretold of David's successor, who would establish His Kingdom of justice and peace forever.

Agape motivated Jesus to leave glory to inhabit human flesh, walk on earth for thirty-three years, and share His message of love, faith, and redemption. He healed the sick, raised the dead, fed the hungry, encouraged the downtrodden, and taught a most captivating and distinct message.

He showed exceptional love to His betrayer, Judas, who attended His last Passover Seder. He could have exposed or condemned him, but He did not. Instead, He gave Judas permission to betray Him, "That thou doest, do quickly." (John 13:27) Although Judas did not recognize it until it was too late to turn back, Jesus was offering Judas a last chance to repent. Later, while praying in the Garden of Gethsemane, agape led Jesus to accept His vicarious death on the cross for our redemption. The Disciples were sleeping, and He was praying alone to His Father. He asked His Heavenly Father if it were possible to escape death.

Yet, He chose to fulfill God's will, not His. After being beaten, spat upon, and crowned with thorns, Jesus still surrendered Himself to be stripped naked and nailed to a wooden cross. It's ironic how the Creator allowed us to use His creation: a wooden cross (from trees) and metal spikes (from metal ore) to disgrace and humiliate Him. Such remarkable behavior reveals His unselfish, everlasting love for us.

Sinful humans affixed Jesus to a wooden cross with metal spikes in His hands and feet. Then we placed Him on a hill between two thieves, before throngs of mocking people. Jesus could have commanded legions of angels to destroy us. Yet, He did not. He gave up His life to pay the penalty for sin. *What a wonderful Savior!*

Three days later, He rose from the dead, declaring He had all power in Heaven and earth! His love raised Him from the dead to ascend into Heaven where He intercedes for us before the Father. His love sent us the Holy Spirit to comfort and abide with us while we await Jesus' glorious return. Then we shall know His pure love in its full measure forever. *Hallelujah!*

God's love provides what is best for us. 1 John 4:10 tells us we should never measure love by how much we love God. Instead, we should measure love by how much He loves us, and how He sent His Son to pay sin debt. His unselfish love makes us right before God, as He sees His own amazing grace. Jesus relinquished His deity and glory, not for what we could do for Him, but for what He needed to do for us at Calvary. No longer are we without hope for redemption. God's love lifted us from despair into the presence of God forever as this familiar hymn attests,

Love Lifted Me[26]
James Rowe (1865-1933)

I was sinking deep in sin, Far from the peaceful shore, Very deeply stained within, Sinking to rise no more; But the Master of the sea, Heard my despairing cry, From the waters lifted me– Now safe am I.

All my heart to Him I give, Ever to Him I'll cling, In His blessed presence live, Ever His praises sing. Love so mighty and so true, Merits my soul's best songs; Faithful, loving service, too, To Him belongs.

Souls in danger, look above, Jesus completely saves; He will lift you by His love, Out of the angry waves. He's the Master of the sea, Billows His will obey; He your Savior wants to be– Be saved today.

Refrain:
Love lifted me, Love lifted me, When nothing else could help, Love lifted me; Love lifted me, Love lifted me, When nothing else could help, Love lifted me.

---

[26] James Rowe, "Love Lifted Me," *The New Church Hymnal*, Ralph Carmichael, et al., ed., (Newbury Park: Lexicon Music, 1976) 434.

The Greatest of These Is Love
In 1 John 4:7-8 we read,

> Beloved, let us love one another: for love is of God; and every one that loveth is born of God, and knoweth God. He that loveth not knoweth not God; for God is love.

God showed His love toward us, and He empowers us to share it as we forgive, reconcile, and extend ourselves. This is the "most excellent way" we read in 1 Corinthians 13 (*Love Chapter*).

This unselfish love is patient and kind. It is always at work, seeking opportunities to show kindness on our behalf when we are ready to receive. This love is not jealous, boastful, proud, or rude. Possessiveness or irritability is never present, because the giver does not care about what the recipient can do "to deserve it." Then it's no longer love; it's a loan.

Love does not demand its own way; it is not irritable and keeps no record of wrongs. It doesn't keep score, as do so many who've offended others and need seek forgiveness themselves. Love is not glad about injustice, but is glad when truth prevails. Love never gives up, it never loses faith, it is ever hopeful, and it endures. Of these three, faith, hope, and love, the greatest of these is love.

Love is practical, as we extend benevolence and forgiveness toward others,

> To forgive someone is to admit our limitations. God's given us only one piece of life's jigsaw puzzle. Only God has the cover of the box. To forgive someone is to display reverence. Forgiveness is not saying the one who hurt you was right. Forgiveness is stating that God is fair and he will do what is right. After all, don't we have enough things to do without trying to do God's work too? [27]

It's easy to love when someone reciprocates it. Relationships fail when we cannot show love that covers a multitude of faults. Death is the ultimate price that one can pay to show love. Christ did that for us, and His divine love extends mercy and forgiveness to us all. We emulate God's perfect love by forgiving others' wrongdoings, showing mercy, and extending goodwill. When we express this Christ-like love, we can live right in the eyes of God and humanity.

In God's eyes, we are His obedient children who express His character. To humanity, we reflect God's love and show we belong to His Son, Jesus Christ. With love, our Christian faith becomes an attractive alternative to any life outside of Christ.

Our Lord lived it from the beginning, and He will complete this perfect work in us. Faith makes us

---

[27] Max Lucado, *When God Whispers Your Name* (Dallas: Word Publishing, 1994), 94.

receptacles of God's grace and mercy, and His Spirit fills us with virtue. We get knowledge, exercise temperance, patience, godliness, and brotherly kindness. However, love shows the unselfish heart of God.

In this chapter, we explored love. Before going to the Epilogue, read the following scenario where you have to make a moral decision. Once you've read the account, please compare your answers to those in the Appendix.

Abiding in Love
You interview to be director of a youth program. The board chair offers you the position with the promise to supply you with details when you report in two weeks. You pack your things and move closer to the organization. The day before you report to work, the board secretary informs you they will not hire you, and you take a part-time job to pay the bills.

Six months later, the director makes a ministry presentation to recruit volunteers at the church you attend. You volunteer to tutor troubled teens with their math and English twice a week. The organization will recognize you with a volunteer service plaque next month for fifteen years of volunteer service, during which you have befriended and supported the director faithfully.

Scenario Questions: Was this the proper response? What would you have done? Why?

Epilogue

Epilogue
Not I, But Christ

One Saturday

It was a sunny afternoon on my first visit to prison. I was one of many church volunteers from area experienced in church and community "lay ministry." As prison ministry novices, we were the "blind leading the blind." Yet, our passion for sharing the Lord with His "least of these" (Matthew 25:40) convinced us that despite our inexperience, the Lord used our efforts to bring Him glory.

The prison denied our access initially because I wore denim, which was unauthorized since it looked like inmate clothing. After changing into overalls (provided by the prison), they allowed us inside. The officers escorted us to an outdoor reception area within the compound, where we assembled with about four to six inmates. We spent the rest of the day in worship and fellowship. We read the Scriptures, prayed, sang songs, shared testimonies, and chatted together.

The experience shattered my assumptions and preconceptions that inmates were not "monsters." They were human beings worthy of our love and respect. *Koinonia* (Chapter Seven) can happen in the most desolate areas, facilitated by God's Spirit. I learned inmates are not ignorant of Scripture, desperate for my "great" knowledge. Many of them are astute Bible students, capable of quoting and explaining Scripture effectively. (The

Scriptures are not sterile and irrelevant; they are the living Words of God we can use in any situation.) I learned another profound lesson that day from Galatians 2:20, *"I live; yet not I, but Christ liveth in me!"* These inspiring words of sacrifice and commitment have resonated within my heart.

Over the Years

Once, a pastor challenged me to use my mind constructively for the Kingdom, which ultimately begged this question, "If I were to give myself to the Lord completely, living according to the Bible, and trusting Him to fulfill His wonderful promises—*what could happen for this poor black kid from the projects?"*

Some would contend that I am a hopeless and helpless product of a "systemically racist" society, and that because of my impoverished past environment, social status, and skin color, I will always be a "victim." Thus, I should subscribe to the "system of victimization" paradigm and accept a life that is "inferior," "disadvantaged," and/or "predisposed to crime and/or failure."

However, as a youth, I realized two things. First, I saw how my race was not the only victim to hatred or prejudice. Besides the biblical examples prejudice between Jew and Gentile or Jew and Samaritans, there were historical examples of how we mistreated the Native Americans; how the Hitler Regime mistreated the Jews, and how we mistreated the Japanese in the US during WWII.

I also noted how blacks, whites, and other races expressed hatred toward people within their own race, which I found quite curious. From these experiences, I learned that sin is the only "systemic" racial problem, which causes *all* people to hate and pre-judge indiscriminately.

Second, I realized that despite how society would classify me, my Everlasting Creator and Redeemer makes no such distinction. He is "no respecter of persons" (Acts 10:34-35), and He loves *all* His Children—including me—equally. Thus, He gives me the freedom and grace to live a morally responsible life, consistent with His perfect will.

The Lord used my racial, cultural, and societal circumstances to fulfill His excellent work, which far surpassed anything I could have planned for myself. I just needed to trust in Him enough to, as another Christian once told me, *"Let go and let God!"*

Therefore, I differ with those who trivialize the Christian faith as a "pie-in-the-sky" religion. Mine has been a life of abundance (John 10:10), which began the moment I met the Lord and will continue forever. Only He gives my life its purpose and meaning while supplying me with fulfillment and satisfaction.

My life has not been about keeping the rules and rituals associated with a stereotyped religious practice. Instead, I have an intimate, personal relationship with a loving friend and companion. Thus, I've tried to answer the pastor's question by not depending on my gifts and ability alone. Jesus Christ needs to occupy the center of everything I desire in life, as He orders and delights in every step I take,

> The steps of a good man are ordered by the LORD: and he delighteth in his way. Though he fall, he shall not be utterly cast down: for the LORD upholdeth him with his hand. I have been young, and now am old; yet have I not seen the righteous forsaken, nor his seed begging bread. (Psalm 37:23-25)

Although my being a "good" man has been questionable, He remains loving, patient, kind, and faithful in all things. In John 16:33, the Lord tells us to be of good cheer because He overcame the world's challenges successfully—including an inhumane death on a Roman cross. Therefore, my victory is in Him.

The Next Step

At this phase in life, my self-centered plans yield to Christ-centered, God-honoring, and Bible-based ones. I desire to finish well in furthering the Kingdom by living out the principles of Psalm 92:14,

> They shall still bring forth fruit in old age;
> they shall be fat and flourishing.

I will never "arrive" at total spiritual and moral completion in this life. I am still learning and growing. Yet, I have a wonderful example in Christ, who pledges His support and power that enables me to serve Him. I am amazed at how He guides me so precisely. The more I live, the more I experience His eternal truth,

> For all the promises of God in him are yea, and in him Amen, unto the glory of God by us. (2 Corinthians 1:20)

I do not know what the future holds, but I know who holds it in His caring hands. He is always with me, watching over me—even when I'm not aware of His presence and providence. I am astounded at how the Lord continues to "show Himself strong" (2 Chronicles 16:9), especially during those dark times of uncertainty and weakness. I deserve God's wrath and condemnation. My works can never engender boasting since before Christ they were filthy rags, and after Christ they become the mundane tasks my Master expects of me. (Isaiah 64:6, Luke 17:7–10)

I can never be "good enough" to earn His consideration. Yet, I can continue pressing toward the heavenly prize awaiting all those who love His appearing. (Philippians 3:14, 2 Timothy 4:8) This is all He requires. My life has been exceptional. The "outer man" continues to decay, but the "inner man" is renewing daily. (2 Corinthians 4:16) For this, I am eternally grateful.

What a wonderful Savior!

Appendices

Appendix A
Suggested Christian Heritage Code

Faith is the foundation of my new life in Christ. Through **virtue**, I have the moral strength to live and act circumspectly before others, as I use my **knowledge** to share God's Word adroitly as His Spirit draws others to Him. The Lord can satisfy my physical and emotional needs through **temperance**. As I yield to and obey Him, I can respond to temptation properly.

God's limitless power helps me endure **patiently** while He displays His **godliness** to attract others to Him. The marvel of **brotherly kindness** gives me the means to treat other Christians as His redeemed people who will share eternity together with Christ. The wonder of **love** releases me from selfishness to express benevolence to a fallen world, revealing that I belong to Jesus. With these eight characteristics, I can help make this world a better place to live.

Appendix B
Suggested Scenario Answers

Chapter Two: A Problem with Money
Scenario: A friend gives you an anonymous cash donation of 1.5 million dollars for your organization, which is having financial difficulty.

Answer: You give the entire donation to your organization. Laws that govern charitable giving apply to anonymous donations as well.

Chapter Three: Double Trouble
Scenario: Because of your employer's misdeeds, you go to prison. During chapel service, the chaplain invites you to share your testimony before the congregation.

Answer: You share of God's goodness and faithfulness—even during times of distress. God is sovereign and is always at work for us.

Chapter Four: What's It Worth?
Scenario: You will succeed your CEO at the company's annual meeting, where he's planned for you to meet a friend for sex during the three-day meeting.

Answer: You decline the sex offer because it tarnishes your Christian witness and imperils your walk with the Lord.

Chapter Six: For the Sake of the Call
Scenario: Someone offers to advance your ministry if you leave your family for them immediately.

Answer: God will expand your work and preserve your marriage and family. The Bible teaches we must preserve and protect them, because no advancement is worth that sacrifice.

Chapter Seven: A True Friend
Scenario: A couple responsible for your being fired at one church come to another church where you pastor. They are without, so you give them money, help them get housing and employment, and your families become friends.

Answer: The Christian family seeks to forgive and forget offenses since Christ has forgiven and forgotten our offenses. Ours was the correct response.

Chapter Eight: Abiding in Love
Scenario: The organization that recruited but did not hire you recruits you to volunteer tutor troubled kids and you consent. They will recognize you for fifteen years of service.

Answer: The Lord wants us to love and forgive unconditionally without harboring grudges or expressing ill will. Ours was the correct response.

About the Author

Floyd Bland has served as elder, teacher, chaplain, and administrator to help others grow in their faith through sound, practical, Bible-based models for Christian living.

His other books include *Radical Forgiveness Through the Eyes of Jesus, Five Things Every Christian Must Know, Oh For The Joy! Forgiven and Free in Christ, and The Last Words of Jesus to His Disciples: Enduring Lessons of Faith, Hope, and Love.*

Floyd married his best friend and helpmate. Together, they have two grown children and a grandson.